3995
17.00

THE FEARLESS HORSE

Roger & Joanna Day

David and Charles

A DAVID & CHARLES BOOK
Copyright © David & Charles Limited 2006

David & Charles is an F+W Publications Inc. company
4700 East Galbraith Road
Cincinnati, OH 45236

First published in the UK in 2006

ISBN-13: 978-0-7153-2370-0 hardback
ISBN-10: 0-7153-2370-9 hardback

Printed in China by RR Donnelley
for David & Charles
Brunel House   Newton Abbot   Devon

Commissioning Editor Jane Trollope
Editor Jennifer Proverbs
Designer Jodie Lystor
Production Controller Beverley Richardson
Project Editor Jo Weeks

Visit our website at www.davidandcharles.co.uk

David & Charles books are available from all good bookshops; alternatively
you can contact our Orderline on 0870 9908222 or write to us at FREEPOST EX2 110,
D&C Direct, Newton Abbot, TQ12 4ZZ (no stamp required UK only); US customers call
800-289-0963 and Canadian customers call 800-840-5220.

*Horse care and riding are not without risk, and minors should be supervised by an adult
at all times; while the authors and publishers have made every attempt to offer accurate and
reliable information to the best of their knowledge and belief, it should be followed only
by those with prior equestrian knowledge and experience, and is presented without any
guarantee. The authors and publishers therefore disclaim any liability incurred in connection
with using the information contained in this book.
It is advisable to wear protective headgear whenever working with horses.*

CONTENTS

INTRODUCTION

Between us, my husband Roger and I have almost 100 years of successful and practical experience in producing and training competition horses, including breeding Primmore's Pride. Since we sold him as a foal, this amazing horse has won more world class three-day events than any other in the world today, including Kentucky, Burghley, Badminton, an Olympic team silver and individual bronze medal, and helped his rider, Pippa Funnell, win the Rolex Grand Slam. His dam was our horse of a lifetime, Primmore Hill, grand dam of 'The Colt', whose trials and tribulations are the inspiration for this book.

⇧ Roger, Joanna and Pippa Funnell, all so proud of homebred Primmore's Pride, an amazing brave and generous horse, here after winning Burghley 2003 and the Rolex Grand Slam

⬆ A great team – Roger jumping Tigger, the 'unrideable' horse, team chasing (c1980)

⬆ Joanna show jumping Quail in Grade C championships (c1968) – a real trier

Although from very different backgrounds, Roger and I both grew up on farms among horses and have ridden from childhood. At 17 I began my classical British Horse Society education. I trained briefly at Talland gaining my BHSAI then spent a couple of years training show jumpers in Belgium before I returned to the Yorkshire Riding Centre and enjoyed a superb classical dressage education from Nicole Bartle.

After moving to Somerset to help set up a new training establishment, and successfully gaining my BHSI, I fell in love with and married a dashing young hunting farmer, Roger Day. We married in 1972 and continued farming while also training horses and riders to become successful competitors in many spheres, particularly eventing. I also evented successfully until a serious neck injury in 1979 ended my competitive career. Roger excelled at team chasing and hunter trials, especially with his beloved 'unrideable' Tigger the Tiger, infamous as 'that biscuit-coloured hoss'. He also joined the Taunton Vale Foxhounds each Friday, boldly showing the way over the big hedges and ditches on a variety of the 'tricky' horses that passed through our hands.

The Colt – From Fearsome Foe to Fearless Horse

The Colt was a handsome foal and very cocky too, like all the foals from the great Primmore line. As was our usual custom, he was offered for sale at weaning and duly delivered to his new home just before we went on holiday. On our return we realized the cheque had not cleared so we set off to collect him and found, to our horror, an emaciated, virus-riddled sad little chap.

Feeling very ashamed that we had allowed such a fate to befall him, we took him home and nursed him through his illness. As he got stronger and bigger, he became more and more vicious for no apparent reason. Like most traditional horsemen at that time, we had no other tools except dominance, force and inflicting pain to try to control him: we got tougher and tougher, but he just got angrier and angrier until even two strong men with leading poles couldn't manage to get him to the paddock.

We couldn't work out why The Colt was so vicious as all his siblings had been testing but kind. We had him gelded but it made no noticeable difference. Eventually, after consulting many experts, we decided that the kindest thing was to have him put down, even though he was only three years old. He was just too dangerous to keep on a farm, especially one full of

⬆ The Colt, alias Primmore's Pompous, ready for the High Performance Sales as an unweaned foal

⇧ We believed he was a hopeless case

⇧ The Colt was prepared to fight off any tigers

⇩ A fearsome foe

holidaymakers, which was how we earned our living then. By chance, I attended a natural horsemanship demonstration and although I was very sceptical of what I witnessed, I decided to invite one of the trainer's students to the farm to see if he could do anything to help The Colt. The student turned out to be a slightly-built, gentle young man called Adam Goodfellow – we feared The Colt would eat him for breakfast! To our amazement, however, Adam quickly and quietly improved The Colt's behaviour, gaining some trust and respect in a remarkably short time.

The techniques of pressure and release that Adam used proved to be so effective that despite our years of experience, we became enthusiastic students again. This was the beginning of an amazing journey discovering all the different, and at times conflicting, more natural methods of horsemanship. Eventually we stumbled on some brilliant Australian and Canadian dressage and jumping trainers who made practical sense of it all. They, and other leading competition trainers who also incorporate these principles, inspired enough confidence in us to begin using these techniques in our professional work.

By adding some of their communication methods to our traditional ones, we formulated our own training approach, which we call Effective Training. The principles and concepts, techniques and strategies of this approach are the subjects of this book, and they can be used for working with a variety of horses and

⇧ Gradually, The Colt began to show some trust and respect

⇩ The Colt testing the leadership

⇩ Working in harmony – Effective Training transforms The Colt

like his siblings, but has to make do with teaching Effective Training techniques and performing at demos where he is living up to his real name Primmore's Pompous. He has come from being the dreaded Fearsome Horse to the adored Fearless Horse!

As well as explaining our Effective Training approach, this book is a tribute to The Colt's courage and persistence in demonstrating his confusion, his forgiving generosity in allowing us to regain his trust, and latterly his expressiveness and patience in teaching people how to communicate in a manner that horses can easily understand. Now middle-aged, this impressive black gelding is our beloved schoolmaster, showing people of all ages and stages how to safely manage a big volatile horse. He demonstrates admirably that it is the way in which the human approaches the horse that determines how the horse will respond. This book would not have been written without The Colt and his on-going journey to becoming the Fearless Horse.

riders of any age, size, type, standard or discipline. Based on very clear communication and understanding the horse's point of view, this approach has proved extremely successful even with the ever-challenging Colt, as well as with a wide variety of clients and their horses.

Through The Colt's emotional progress and our greatly increased effectiveness as trainers, we gradually developed a relationship of trust and respect instead of fear and anger. Our newfound understanding of what The Colt was trying to tell us through his behaviour led us to realize that damage caused to his joints (DJD) by the virus he contracted as a foal meant he was in a great deal of discomfort. Once again we consulted yet more experts – the conclusion was that he would never be able to compete, which was what he was bred to do. Despite this, because of what we had already been through with him, and the positive things he had taught us, to say nothing of his courage and beauty, we felt we owed it to him to give him yet another chance. The long uncertainty over his future is why this horse is still called just 'The Colt'.

We have kept on carefully building up his work and schooling and he has regular check-ups, special shoes and chiropractic and acupuncture treatments. Although often not sound, he gets stronger and more beautiful, both physically and emotionally, every year. He should have been a world-class competition horse,

⤴ Developing the fearless – bombproof – pony

A long way to go?

It can be difficult to employ new horsemanship methods in your work with your own horse, especially if you have always managed adequately with traditional and classical techniques. However, look at it another way, Effective Training aims to communicate with horses in their own language, and while it is only human to want to converse in our own language, many of the world's greatest leaders have been fluent in many languages, particularly of those of the people with whom they wanted to form good partnerships. And so it could be with your relationship with your horse – learn something about how he communicates to improve your partnership together. Overcome your apprehension and give this way of working a try. You should find Effective Training opens up opportunities for you to develop an expressive confident horse that is going willingly forward yet remains safe and rideable in all situations, a great partner – the fearless horse or pony!

Training is usually divided into levels, but in reality a sliding scale of progress should be maintained, from the raw recruit to highly educated horse. This book

aims to pass on some of the things we have learned in our continuing search for better horsemanship. It will show you how to develop a good sense of feel and timing, which will help make you a consistently better leader. It is no easy task, but will be worthwhile, whether you use your improved communication skills on humans or horses.

Learning the approach we explain in this book will be like learning any new skill. You may want to find out just a little to be safer in your every day dealings with your horse, or just enough for basic communication, or you may be keen to master Effective Training in greater depth and gain the ability to start youngsters, or to train or even retrain any horse to be safe, rideable and fearless.

Every effort to learn his language will be appreciated by your horse: he himself is absolutely fluent in the use of body language to communicate, and a very good teacher – if you take the time to allow him to teach you. Inevitably you will make lots of mistakes, and just as you should allow your horse the freedom to learn from his mistakes, you should allow yourself the same leniency. Horses are unbelievably forgiving and uncritical, generously letting you try again

MAKE AND TAKE TIME

A fearless safe rideable horse is just what we all want. But how? The answer is simple – good training of yourself and your horse! Good training requires forward planning and time for learning and schooling. How are you going to find the time? My way is to be sure that I do make time to do the things that only I can do. For example, only I can teach myself to communicate

politely put on his bridle – that has to prove quicker in the end.

Go the whole way. Find enough time to train yourself to overcome your natural predatorial instincts of 'do what I say or else'. Once you start to use good leadership instead of dominance, your horse will learn to overcome his natural prey animal instincts of flight or fight. Together you can learn to respect and trust each other and become a successful

⇧ One of Jim Wright's herd of horses running free in the lush Matahura Valley in New Zealand

◁ Developing a trusting partnership

better with horses, only I can build my partnership with my horse, only I can school him to respond to my aids and agree where our 'buttons' are (see p.42). Anyone can do the chores! Your horse doesn't care how smart his yard is but he does care about having company, water, food, shelter, stimulus and exercise. He loves to learn to use his athleticism and skills to show off, if this is done within a good partnership, safely and with plenty of fun included.

Think before you make any excuses. I meet people who say they can't make the time for schooling. Is it really quicker to go and fetch a chair to stand on and battle with the horse with his head in the rafters every time they want to put on his bridle? It should take only 2–6 five-minute Effective Training sessions to teach him to lower his head and wait confidently while you

partnership. We want to train our horses to remain trusting and gentle in all sorts of situations that are totally unnatural for them, just as you would need special training if you were to survive unaided in their natural environment.

Begin at the beginning with an end goal in mind and break the journey down into small achievable lessons. Even if you are not intending to keep him for long, train every horse as though you were building a partnership for life. Teach him as carefully as a good boss trains a new recruit; equip him with all the skills and knowledge he needs to be a brilliant and trustworthy P.A. You will be rewarded with a well-educated, confident and trustworthy partner, able to cope with anything the world throws at him.

◁ Riding should be fun

◁ 'Of course.' Primmore's Patience politely moves her feet for me

Rebuilding confidence with show jumps before moving on to jumping them

and again, but they are also so appreciative when you eventually get it right!

We would like to stress that you do not need to be superhuman to do this work, but you do need to care, and you do need to become well co-ordinated and fairly agile. Roger and I are not sound, not young, not fit, not strong and yet by using our Effective Training techniques and strategies we can help the most unmanageable horses to become gentle and confident.

How to use this book

With its well-illustrated instructional text, this book is intended to be very practical. The idea is that you will feel confident enough to have a go – with the book propped up on the fence, if necessary! Even if you are simply looking for some troubleshooting, we recommend that you read the rest of the book first and start by working through the Effective Training exercises (p.54–113). Through doing this schooling, most difficulties will vanish and your troubles will be over. The training is mostly about your approach to horses and you do not need to do every single exercise every day with every horse. Once you have

trained a horse through each exercise, he should only need the occasional revision as required. The exercises are suitable for horses or humans of any age shape or size and please do take 'him', 'he' or 'horseman' to also refer to 'her' 'she' and 'horsewoman' throughout.

We dream of finding this book on kitchen, tackroom, or horsebox tables, consulted by all: riders, trainers, grooms, students, clients, fathers, mothers and megastars. Hopefully, you will all become so inspired that you will want to learn much more, not only from us, but also from the many other caring teachers and trainers, new and old, who have offered up their knowledge to help you become a better horseman or horsewoman.

Good luck!

Gentle and kind. The Colt – transformed – respectfully allows our two-year-old grandaughter to hold him as we look on to supervise

PROTECT ABUSED HORSES

In making such effective training methods widely available our only worry is that if they fall into the wrong hands they could be used to abuse horses. However, we are reassured by our belief that the majority of people reading this book are trying to be good horsemen. If you see anyone being cruel to a horse – or any living thing – please take appropriate and effective action to prevent it or report them to the relevant authority.

EFFECTIVE TRAINING

'If it is good, it is easy!' This valuable saying explains so much about training and how your horse should feel: if you and the horse are working well and finding it easy, that is good training, but if it is a struggle that is poor training. This phrase was taught to me in the late 1970s by a young Dutch trainer Henk Van Bergen, now one of the best dressage trainers in the world. Whenever Roger and I are teaching or working with a horse or rider, we keep this saying in the back of our minds.

Our aim is to make our Effective Training approach easy to understand and very rewarding – for both horse and human. So that you can give it a try and find out for yourself, this section begins by explaining a little about what makes horses tick and how we can use their natural instincts to help improve our working relationship with them. It goes on to outline the key skills you need to use to help your horse understand what you want from him, and to help him learn to trust you enough to give you what you want. At the end of the section, a glossary demystifies any jargon and recaps on any important terms.

BEFORE YOU BEGIN... REMEMBER

Freedom of choice offers opportunities for learning and decision-making; good education leads to good decision-making. During all your work, remember to allow yourself and your horse the chance to learn by getting things right and wrong, and then to correct mistakes by changing your minds. This freedom of choice develops confidence and self-control.

⬆ The freedom to learn self-control

⬆ Henk Van Bergen riding Primmore Hill while teaching Joanna, who has an injured neck, at a clinic in 1980

⇧ If it's good, it's easy

Communication – look, listen and learn how to notice and understand what your horse is saying

Horses are never silent. Every minute he is with you, your horse is trying to communicate with you. Horses use their voices only as a greeting or warning, so they cannot understand our words, but can recognize our call as they would another horse's whinny, and can learn to understand the implication of the tone of our voice. Horses express themselves entirely through their body language, the way they move and their facial expressions, their snorts and sighs as well as their tail carriage.

• A horse is always honest

Horses are incapable of lying to you, hiding their feelings, being deceitful or plotting to aggravate you. They are simply not able to think, for example, I know she wants me to do a half pass, so I will be really annoying and flex the other way. They do not have that

⬆ Non-verbal communication galore. Roger reassures Charlie who with head up and ribs out shows anxiety about the larger horses. Whiskers, on the right, shows interest, unlike Passion, on the left, who flicks a 'go away' tail and flexes away from the group

LISTEN TO YOUR HORSE

Remember, during all the training you do, your horse will tell you how he is feeling. Watch him and fine-tune your interpretation skills. When you pause in your work, step away from your horse's head and look for him bowing. When he bows, if he lowers his head and keeps it there with gentle eyes that is a good sign and means he is relaxed; he may also lick and chew. However, if he blinks a lot or shuts his eyes it probably means he is finding it hard work, that you are in danger of over-facing him and he is beginning to shut down. If he bows his head and puts it straight back up again he is nervous of you.

If you get no bowing or licking and chewing, you are probably just standing too close and working too fast: give him time and space to communicate with you. It is important that the horse bows to you and not you to him. What you are seeking to teach the horse is that it is ok to hand over responsibility for his safety to you and trust your leadership. He needs to build confidence that you will take care of him and learn to ignore anything that worries him but which you say is not a threat. Once he accepts this he may well yawn a lot, a sign of handing over responsibility to you.

⬇ Lizzie Pyle allows her 'guinea pig' mare to express herself. As I move away, she bows and licks and chews on cue

Read your horse's face

BOWING – When the horse lowers his head on an outstretched neck to show you respect and trust. He will often simultaneously lick his lips and make chewing movements with his mouth.

CHEWING – A submissive gesture from the horse expressed by moving the mouth as though eating. Australian trainer Mark Rodney refers to this as digesting a thought (see also **LICKING LIPS**).

CHIN – In a horse a tight chin indicates that he is anxious while a soft chin indicates he is relaxed.

type of intelligence. They can be playful or grumpy and have greatly different characteristics but can never be anything but totally honest with you. This is a concept that some readers might find hard to accept because we are so accustomed to mistakenly humanizing our horses, and humans often say one thing but mean another, especially with their body language. Horses *never* do this and find this human trait impossibly confusing.

Horses love to please and try their hardest to do what you ask. If they are being difficult or 'stubborn', it is because they are finding us difficult to understand, respect or trust. However, if a horse thinks you might be threatening his survival, he will resist, especially if you use force. A horse that has become desensitized, has been abused or over-faced can also be very resistant to change because he is reluctant to repeat his 'mistakes', but please don't let this put you off. Look at it from his point of view – what's in it for him? Few horses cease to try to express their feelings, even after years of being misunderstood (if only humans were always that totally straightforward) so have a go at showing him you will listen and he will quickly open up and begin to communicate with you.

Horses can feel angry, depressed or happy, but always as a result of a prior event, not in anticipation of the future. For example, they can be happy to be led out to the paddock, but not sad or aware that they will soon be brought in again. However, they can anticipate something through close association: for example, being led to the field means freedom, or being loaded into a lorry means they're going somewhere. And they can get anxious because of such associations, but if they are confident in what they anticipate will be happening, they will remain cool and calm – this applies especially when preparing for travelling or competing.

It is important to realize that horses can easily pick up on our emotions; they sense when we are excited, angry, sad or happy and respond accordingly.

FROZEN WATCHFULNESS – This is when a horse is so nervous of his trainer that he never takes his eyes off him. It is often seen after someone has been working a horse loose and unintentionally frightened it by chasing it around. Unfortunately, sometimes people think they have 'join up', but although it looks similar, it is different because it is a lack of trust that makes the horse feel the need to know where you are all the time – as he would a predator, especially one that has just been chasing him. A joined up horse can be with you when you invite him and will be happy to move away when not required. A horse needs to be confident enough in your presence to feel happy to leave you, graze, drink, turn his back to you, wander off, roll, lie down, pee, poo. If he doesn't relax when you are around, you may be making him nervous by being too demanding.

LICKING LIPS – This is a sign of relief but is often thought of as an indication that the horse is digesting a thought because horses often do it when they have just learned something. (See also **CHEWING**.)

NOSES AND NOSTRILS – A wriggling nose means concentration and effort. A blunt nose means relaxation. A tight nose means anxiety or shutdown. Flared nostrils indicate alarm, wrinkled up nostrils indicate offence, while soft nostrils mean the horse is relaxed.

SHUTTING DOWN – This is when a horse withdraws emotionally from outside stimulus and becomes quiet and unresponsive, often with dull eyes, not looking out in to the world.

(For more definitions, see the Glossary, pp.50–53)

◁ Miss Moneypenny tells JP Daker, 'Ask me anything and I'll do it if I can.'

⇧ 'Oh no! What are you going to do next?' Charlie is worried by Rachel

⬆ Whiskers clearly says, 'Shan't go there...'

⬆ 'Well, ok then, if you help me.' Whiskers changes her mind and Jemina thanks her

A HORSE'S SECRET THOUGHTS – HIS BODY LANGUAGE TELLS ALL

Next time you see a horse working, watch his body language. It can tell you all about what he is thinking. A forward but gentle eye, soft ears and mouth and chin are all signs of confidence. Tightness in any of these is a sign of tension in the body or soul of the horse. The truly confident horse will also have a proud but soft tail carriage and any deviation from that ideal is a sure sign of inner troubles, either physical or emotional. Tail swishing often indicates offence at overzealous use of the aids, especially with mares, but it can indicate pain or resentment. It is a shame that it is frequently ignored by dressage judges. A crooked tail is usually a sign of physical problems. Soft concave ribs mean a respectful horse, stiff braced ribs mean a worried or rude horse. Soft athletic footfalls indicate a happy horse, restricted or harsh foot falls mean a resentful horse.

⬆ 'I think there may be a crocodile in there' – look at the tail and ribs. 'No, never fear, I'm here.' Roger gives Whiskers confidence though positive riding

Consequently, if you are in a hurry they may be extra-resistant, not intentionally to annoy you, but because they feel threatened by the urgency in your movements. When feeling trapped or threatened in any way, horses react instinctively with their flight or fight response, which even after years of being with humans is still quickly evident when things go wrong. Maybe it feels as though you are trying to 'capture' them, perhaps by hurriedly cramming on the headcollar, or by doing something you usually don't do, such as tying them up. Try to interpret these activities in the way a horse might, and teach yourself how to behave differently. Learn to distance yourself from his and your emotions when neccessary. Imagine someone arriving at the scene of a crisis. If they become hysterical then you are not going to look to them for help. The person you will turn to is the calm, efficient and effective one, and this is how you need to be with your horse. To be that person, you need to be well organized, relaxed and confident; you also need good leadership skills. Your horse will team up with you, if you make good decisions on his behalf even when things go awry between you or with the outside world.

⬆ Adrenaline flare up – a potential crisis...

⬆ ...is successfully defused by using lateral flexion yields to lower the adrenaline and gentle the horse

• Voice recognition

Although they cannot understand words as such, horses can be trained to the react to the voice by the process of association of an action with a sound. This is often used while riding youngsters, to protect their mouths from being pulled on. For example, a good trainer will use body language (see also p.32), a tug on the neckstrap and the sound 'Whoa' to teach a horse when to stop. This way they do not rely on the rein aid to halt the progress of a struggling young body, already having to adjust to carrying an unaccustomed weight – the rider. Driving horses have to be trained to rely on voice aids, as they cannot see the driver's body language because they are wearing blinkers or the driver is too far behind them.

⬆ 'Walk on boys.' Arkle and Promise at work with Ian Stanford, who farmed with these wonderful Suffolk Punches in Dorset until recently

RESPECT YOUR HORSE

To truly understand horses you need to know and respect their perspective on life and what is important to them. Along with the whiskers, the nose and lips are so sensitive that a horse can feel a tiny pill in a whole bowl of feed and eat everything around it, leaving the pill uneaten! Whiskers help a horse feel where his nose is – remember that a horse cannot see the end of his nose – so that he can avoid getting his head trapped and can tell if he is about to touch something thorny, come up against the electric fencing in the dark and so on. It is important not to trim them off

– it is possible to have an immaculately turned out horse with his whiskers intact. Many show horses are also subjected to the unpleasant experience of having their eyes and noses smeared in cosmetics and baby oil; horses have a very sensitive sense of smell that would be aggravated by the strong fragrances of cosmetics. Although some horses will become accustomed to such smells, they probably all hate it. When you are working with your horse, avoid wearing strong perfume, aftershave or deodorants for the same reason.

⇨ Horse immaculate with whiskers, rider without. JP Daker and Bow House Sydney

Good leadership – how to ensure your horse keeps voting for you

Sir Winston Churchill is reputed to have said, 'If you want to make a good leader of your son then give him horses not wealth.'

To enable your horse to give his very best performance you need him to be offering quality in his work because he wants to please you because he respects you as his elected leader, not just in submission to your dominance. When horses work with desire, you achieve flair instead of subjugation, and although it takes greater skill to acquire, working with a horse like this is artistry. Pure joy! And, you will be consistently more successful in competition. However, horses do not instinctively understand that we are 'intellectually superior', and as far as they are concerned, we have no automatic right to their trust or respect, we are, after all, their natural predator. We cannot force a horse to respect us. Force means dominance, which creates resentment and fear. We need to earn respect by proving we are more consistent and fair than other horses (probably by 'moving the feet'): to use a well-known phrase, we need to be 'a better horse' than they are. This encourages the horse to trust us because we have shown greater leadership skills. Horses like to follow a good leader, which is not necessarily the strongest most dominant horse (or person), but the one that offers them the best chance of survival. Once you prove to your horse how consistently good your leadership is, he will choose to team up with you.

⬆ Miss Moneypenny is willingly offering JP best quality foot movements and a soft forward body

Good leadership also depends on good communication and an understanding of the physiology and psychology of the person or animal involved. With your horse it is just as important that you are able to interpret his signals as it is that he can interpret yours. This is a huge area, and progress in learning about it has occurred recently though increased use of 'natural' techniques. There is no need to do battle with a horse or a person. Once you have understood the strategies and techniques of Effective Training you will be able to negotiate a safe route through any situation, equine or human, business or leisure.

⬆ A simulated start box in preparation for eventing. Caroline is moving Jill's feet in the box to help her to become gentle in confined spaces

Dance partners, a comedian or a trapeze artist need good timing and feel, so does a horseman – these are key to being a good leader. If you think you are not naturally gifted in this area, fear not – you can acquire adequate levels through training and good practice. Your horse may well be your best teacher, but beware – most horses want to train you to allow them to have the leadership role so that they can ensure their own safety, as they see it. As long as they are the leader, they always have the option for fight or flight, and they will practise using these two skills as often as possible to ensure they are well honed. Your job is to reverse the scenario and be a leader who your horse wants to respect and trust. As survival-of-the-fittest behaviour does come naturally to him, you have a lot of work to do to prove you are a worthy leader. Impress him with your superior intelligence, speed of reaction and agility by learning to use your body language and tools fast and well. Show him that survival of the brightest, not just the biggest is the easiest way to prosper. Don't be timid. Once you have decided to do something, do it with conviction, courage and authority. Think of the trumpet player sounding the fanfare. If you are going to make a mistake make sure everyone knows about it!

⬆ Who moves whom? The Colt tries to move Joanna's feet

⬆ Joanna blocks this attempt and The Colt moves his feet. Thank you

• Keep answering his questions

The better the horse, the more often he will check on his leader. It is the survival-of-the-fittest instinct that causes the Beta (horse) to check the Alpha leader (rider) is good enough. This is a never-ending process, whenever you are communicating with any animal or any person. Your horse will check on you by moving a front foot or pushing on the bit or dropping behind the leg.

Providing you notice immediately and react appropriately, he will continue to respect you. Your reactions need to be quick and consistent, easily understood and non-threatening. If he moves a front foot, ask him politely to replace it – thank you! If he pushes on the bit, ask him politely to rebalance and carry himself and you – thank you! If he drops behind the leg, ask him politely to get back up in front of the leg again – thank you!

If he does not respond willingly to your polite requests, you need to ask him more firmly to give what you want and keep up the pressure of the ask until he understands and respects your aid, and gives you the correct response, then release the pressure to reward him. This is why competing is so difficult as there is no chance to go back a few steps

⬆ 'Which way now?' Just checking. Pippa Funnell quickly replies to Primmore's Pride's question

and sort out a misunderstanding while it is brewing: by the time you get that opportunity, the horse may well have been successful in his resistance, causing confusion and leaving you with a problem to sort out. Do reschool any issues as soon as possible, to nip them in the bud. Refrain from competing your horse again until you have the matter sorted. Remember only practising perfection makes perfect, practising mistakes or successful escapes only produces more problems!

• Relinquishing the prey–predator relationship – feet and sight

A horse's main survival tools are his feet and his sight. Winning in competitions is all about persuading your horse to give you total control of his feet – often we ask him to move them in accurate patterns in strange and stressful situations – and we need co-operation and a good partnership with the horse to do this. If you have control of his feet you have control of his life so he needs to feel he can trust you. You have to reassure him that although you may be a predator, you won't eat him – ever. (For how to gain control over your horse's feet, see the exercises pp.60–113.)

If you look at life with humans from a horse's perspective you will begin to understand the natural instincts they have to overcome in order to coexist happily with us. Every horse is very aware of the natural prey–predator relationship he has with humans. While we need to learn to overcome our predatorial behaviour and to communicate with horses in their own language, they, in turn, need to learn to act less instinctively like prey animals, respond to our aids, trust us and accept our strange world. This is how we begin to create a lasting bond – each learning a little of the other's ways.

WHAT'S IN IT FOR HIM?

The best leaders are those who lead by example and listen to their subjects. Bad leaders and dictators expect their subjects to unquestioningly do as they say, and they fight with or kill off the ones who don't. Thankfully, just by looking at this book you have shown you are made of better stuff than that! If you are unsure that your request is fair, try thinking 'What's in it for him? What's in it for me? – the answer should be positive for both of you. Examine your motives before you begin.

⇧ Polite and easy, soft and forward-going. What a good horse

Horses, like many prey animals, have eyes on the side of their head so they can see danger approaching from any angle. They need always to be aware of what is happening around them, which they do by using peripheral vision, so they do not focus on any one thing. Humans have forward-facing eyes that focus on one object at a time. This enables us to be successful hunters. We need to develop our peripheral vision to reassure the horse that we can see what is happening all around us and him, taking responsibility for his safety so he can trust our leadership and not worry about 'tigers' but relax and get on with the job in hand. For example, it is important when riding that we do not look down, but instead look up and around us to give the horse confidence. Without this trust that we will keep him safe, it is hard for the horse to relax, giving the rider control of his head, and flex at the poll because in so doing he loses a lot of peripheral vision.

◁ Preparing for Burghley. JP Daker is asking Bow House Sydney to trust him by moving his feet nearer to the 'tigers' who are clapping and moving umbrellas

◁ JP's eyes should be looking up, checking for 'tigers', so Syd's eyes can be down. Making the most of the chance to walk around the main arena before the dressage at Burghley

YIELDING OR RESISTING – OR SURVIVAL OF THE FITTEST OR BRIGHTEST

Being successful in life – whether equine or human, business or social – is all about deciding when to yield and when to resist. If the 'asker' is not to be trusted and is seeking to damage you then your survival will depend on your ability to resist; if the asker is trustworthy and seeking to help you get on in life, then it's good to yield and accept their leadership. Rider or horse have to decide which course to take, often instantly, and not everyone always makes the right decision, and therein lies the effectiveness and the power of the naturally selective law of survival of the fittest or brightest.

◁ When JP's eyes are down, so Syd's eyes will be up checking for 'tigers' during the competition

Impulsion – a generous gift from your horse to you

Impulsion is an emotionally controlled energy, so it is part of the horse's life-saving system and he will take great care not to waste it. Impulsion can be offered or withdrawn, instantly, at will, by the horse, and he can use it to help, hinder or harm us. We have no right to demand that he gives it to us. Impulsion that is offered with confidence is a prize to be nurtured and appreciated. I liken it to asking someone for a precious possession; when they give it to us, we need to respond appropriately. As a horse gets better at trusting us to be careful with the impulsion he is giving, then asking him for it gets easier too. We can gain part of this trust by not being greedy, only taking what we need and using it with care.

Horses can struggle with controlling their impulsion for a number of reasons. For example, when a green horse responds to a request for impulsion, he may do so inappropriately in a lurch, which will result in him losing his balance. This is where careful training, not gadgets or punishment, is required for him to learn how to maintain his balance and self-carriage with a variety of degrees of impulsion. Horses, such as racehorses, that have never been educated to control their impulsion or their balance, may throw it at you all at once in an uncontrollable mass, which makes them hard to manage. Once educated physically and emotionally, all horses can learn to be balanced, athletic, gentle and therefore polite. If a horse has lost confidence in our trustworthiness because he has

been abused, over-faced or is hurting, then he will withhold his impulsion, and even severe punishment cannot force him to give it. If he has given too much before, he will often keep some back in reserve for himself, in case of a crisis. By retraining using the strategies detailed throughout this book, we can restore these horses' confidence and generosity in everything we ask for.

• The difference between impulsion and adrenaline

Adrenaline is similar to impulsion in that it is a naturally produced substance that creates energy within the body. It is usually produced as a response to something any animal – us included – feels excited by, such as fear or joy. Controlling a horse's adrenaline is difficult but necessary. Reasserting your leadership role by moving his feet will help him calm down. When a horse's adrenaline is raised, he will seem a lot bigger and therefore more intimidating, so by learning to help him lower his adrenaline, you are doing

Styx is resisting and not moving with impulsion. Hannah is responding by using too much leg

A few transitions later and Styx is willingly giving impulsion. Hannah has established herself as his trusted leader

⬆ Exciting moments raise adrenaline. Pippa Funnell and Primmore's Pride on a victory gallop at Badminton

ENERGY AND GENTLENESS

A horse's adrenaline level naturally rises as his energy levels rise; canter creates a higher adrenaline flow than trot, for example. In the wild, canter is only used in a crisis as a horse's instincts tell him that the more quickly he expends his energy, the more danger he is in. Training is aimed towards re-educating his brain as well as his body, so that he can canter or gallop without getting excited (reacting to adrenaline). A horse's self-control develops along with his training so eventually he will remain calm, even when giving maximum effort, such as fully extended in dressage or on the gallops (see p.104). The same principles apply to how he learns to remain calm when there is plenty going on around him, such as at a competition. Effective Training techniques and strategies will enable you to help him achieve this and you will gradually produce a horse that is safe and rideable at all speeds and in all environments.

⬆ Roger riding a grey horse team chasing. The horse is giving huge amount of energy but maintaining a gentle attitude

everyone a favour. I once worked with a wonderful big horse Highland Lad, that could easily fit into his small stable on the show site under normal circumstances, but when he became excited at a prize-giving ceremony, his adrenaline was raised and no way could he get back into that small space. Working in hand, I helped him to lower his adrenaline by moving his feet in turns, circles and lateral movements, eventually asking him to lower his head to graze, and then he realized he could fit back into his stable just fine.

The position of a horse's head is often a good indicator of his adrenaline levels. When his head is up, with ears pricked forwards, he is about to get into flight mode; when his head is down, he is relaxed or sad – a horse grazes with his head down, and he won't graze unless he is calm. The ability to run fast instantly (and therefore possibly save his life) is provided by adrenaline – our aim is to educate the horse to develop control of his instincts and his adrenaline, and its appropriate use.

Your riding skills – developing an independent seat

When you ride your horse it is important to be able to use your body effectively. As the leader it is your responsibility to ensure that your riding skills and knowledge are adequate so that you are not a hindrance to him. Self-balance is crucial to be able to give clear signals to your horse while coping with his movement, reactions, responses and emotions. Developing an independent seat is the most essential skill in good riding. Suppleness and a dressage seat are enhancing but not vital, whereas being able to stay on without hanging on to the horse's mouth or sides is crucial.

⬆ Finding a teacher is not always easy – keep looking until you find someone who helps you learn and boosts your confidence. Lessons should be fascinating and fun, not a bit painful or scary

⬆ Doing 'aeroplanes' improves a young rider's self-balance and self-confidence. Granddad Roger oversees our grandson's early lessons

⬆ Our granddaughter beginning to develop balance on a first ride instead of clutching onto the pony

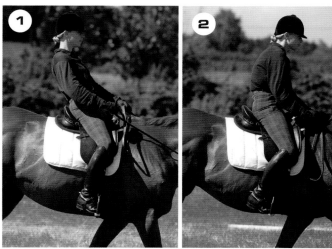

↟ Improving arm and hand position. Joanna demonstrates a soft but heavy elbow with the upper arm perpendicular, which is like a piston, allowing the hand to follow or block the horse's movement, as required

↟ Carrying a stick too high, by the hip, stiffens the hand and arm

↟ A correct seat and softer arm. The elbow is rather straight, which means that the hand is a little low. A very good stick position enabling it to be used with the leg when required

◁ 1) An unbalanced rider leaning back and falling behind the horse's movement
2) An unbalanced rider tipping forward and falling in front of the horse's movement
3) An unbalanced rider whose back is stiff and hollow and so is unable to move with the horse
4) Perfect – a rider in self-balance, allowing the horse freedom of movement. Ear, shoulder, hip, heel in a perpendicular line

Make time to educate and train yourself to be easily in self-balance at all times. Take lunge lessons and learn how to remain in balance while riding without holding the reins, and progress to riding without hanging on to anything. A correct seat is always in self-balance, what is called an independent seat, which means that if your horse suddenly dissolved into thin air you would still be upright and balanced.

The key to an independent seat is maintaining the alignment of the shoulder, hip and heel, regardless of stirrup length. When sitting in the saddle, the ear, shoulder, hip and heel should be in perpendicular alignment; when rising or standing, the hip and heel should be aligned and the knee and toe also. Practise this with a wooden saddle horse or a mechanical horse before you try on a live horse!

⇩ ⇧ Julie and Konker doing a good balanced and sending forward rising trot with the rider's hips opening well. Chin up, Julie!

⇧ Well balanced riders do not hinder their horses at all

⬆ Daisy shows a good jumping position with plenty of weight in the stirrups and good arm, elbow and knee positions allowing Flo to bascule (round) over the jump. It is important to keep everything the same when jumping – not pull more, nor less, not drop the contact, nor tip forward onto the neck. Any of these will unsettle the horse and make his task more difficult

A rider should remain upright and central at all times on turns and circles, allowing their shoulders to turn with the horse's shoulders and their hips with his hips. The rider's legs should hang easily at the horse's side just touching the hair and either blocking or allowing energy to come through as required (see p.45). On a bend, the inside leg should be close to the girth to ask for flexion and the outside leg should be behind the girth to ask for control of the hindquarters. The arms should hang loosely perpendicular from shoulder to elbow unless the hands are moved for some reason. The elbows through to forearms, soft wrists and rounded hands should move in alignment in a fluid straight line to the horse's mouth like pistons, the reins held between thumb and forefinger, in rounded soft fists with bent thumbs on top in a clasp that would keep a sparrow safe, and the reins controlled with soft fourth fingers. The elbows, arms and body allow or block the forward flow of energy.

⬆ Daisy and Gregory demonstrate a good canter turn with both horse and rider upright (not leaning in) and well-balanced

Equipment – you are your best training tool

'It's not the equipment that trains the horse but the hand that holds it,' say the old masters. On the ground and in the saddle the best training tool of all is you, particularly your body language. You can produce a huge range of 'expressions' with your body just as you can with your face. Once you have learnt how to express yourself fluently and control situations, you will feel much more confident, just as you would when becoming fluent in any other 'language'. The hardest part is getting your body to do what you want it to do, and responding fast enough. With Effective Training, you will develop a good line in strange manoeuvres and horse-like behaviour, so it's best to practise with just your horse as the audience, unless you are lucky enough to have another understanding human to experiment on. These body statements and signals (aids) become your common language. (For more information, see pp.32–35.)

• Other tools

There are other tools that can make you more effective and seem impressive – bigger, faster and quicker – to the horse. All are for use as extensions of your body, so the horse needs to learn to trust them as part of you. They need to be used fairly and consistently, and the horse must be trained to understand and respond to them in an educated way. These tools must never be used unpredictably as weapons or instruments of torture to administer punishment, inflict pain or cause distrust. Remember it is the handler that trains, not the tools, so expensive equipment will not make you instantly a better trainer but to be a good workman you need good tools.

⬇ Passion wears a correctly fitted halter over her bridle. The noseband of the halter sits below the bit and is small enough to fit snugly

⬆ Whisky is modelling a knotted halter correctly fitted so that the back of the halter cannot be pulled into her mouth. Tie the knot as shown, otherwise it may gradually loosen and come undone

We use a knotted cord halter for groundwork because it gives an accurate feel for the horse. Such halters are inexpensive and widely available. The knots

WHAT NOT TO USE

Pressure halters that do not release the pressure quickly and easily enough. If the material they are made of is not slippery enough, they can get stuck with the pressure on and produce bad timing and therefore bad training by failing to release at the right moment. Some pressure halters have metal studs on the poll to hurt the horse and should be avoided – it is good timing of the release that trains the horse, not pain. Other pressure headcollars are very complicated and squeeze the head, which is incomprehensible to the horse.

Traditional standard lead ropes, 2m (6ft) long, are not long enough and can encourage problems (see p.119). It is also best to avoid thin lines and ropes that can trap your fingers or very thick ropes, which can become too heavy.

Lead rope clips that require two hands to operate. These are impractical, especially if you have nervous horses to handle.

Whippy sticks that sting. Our training approach works on applying pressure not causing pain. The stick is just an extension of the trainer's arm.

are specifically placed on pressure points that educate the horse for riding aids; for example, the knots on the side prepare for yielding to the bit. You can ride in them too – Western-style, one-rein riding is very good for honing your skills. Standard headcollars are perfect for tying up and travelling horses and fine for the stable yard but too insensitive for the more subtle communication needed when schooling.

When fitting a knotted halter, it is important to secure it properly (see photo, left) and be sure the chin piece cannot get into the horse's mouth. When using one over a bridle we leave the noseband below the bit so that the reins can easily be secured into the throat out of harm's way (see photo, bottom left). Knotted halters will not break so never turn out or tie up in one, use a standard headcollar instead.

A well-fitted light lunging cavesson is a good tool for lunging as it controls the horse from the front of his nose, removing any chance of him carrying his head tilted. Be sure the horse respects your space first and doesn't try to bash you with it. Dually 'Monty Roberts' headcollars with their slide-through nose pieces are great for leading and riding bridleless, but not recommended to tie up the horse. Richard Maxwell makes an excellent slip halter that is very useful for leading and loading and fits easily over a

⬆ The Colt wears a Dually halter, which needs to be carefully fitted with the slide-through noseband sitting well up on the 'frame' of the horse's nose

⬇ Whisky models a well fitted lunging cavesson, which is particularly useful when lunging for exercise if the knotted halter tends to rub

⬆ Gentling a horse to accept rope near his legs. This is a useful lesson if he gets a foot in stockwire as he will wait to be rescued rather than pulling away and injuring himself

bridle or headcollar, but again is unsuitable for tying up. Other items – sheepskin nosebands and neoprene nose, poll and chin protectors – are useful when using nylon halters on thin-skinned or sensitive horses.

You will also need a good rope, about 4m (12ft) long, of medium weight and size. Choose one with 'life' in it, which you can send a 'flick' down (see 'Ropework', p.53) – 14–16mm (½in) sailing rope is excellent. It is readily available from ship's chandlers and is inexpensive. You can attach a trigger clip to one end. Make sure any lead rope clip is not so heavy that it can swing about and hit the horse on the chin or mouth and that it is easy to operate with only one hand. Best quality thick webbing lunge lines can suffice, especially if they are dampened to add weight and life.

PROTECT YOURSELF

My advice for a long and healthy life is to wear a protective hat and gloves, as well as good boots, whenever you are working with horses, even on the ground and in hand. A hard hat will protect your teeth, too, should you get accidentally 'donked' on the head, which happened to me once, cracking all my front teeth. Hard hats can be useful with rude horses that push their head into your face, knowing it is your most vulnerable area; you can simply 'donk' them back and create more respect for the space around your head.

⬇ Use a crash helmet to 'donk' a horse that is trying to push into your head or face

A non-whippy stick about 1.2m (4ft) long with a loop put in the end to which you can attach a 2m (6ft) string or nylon cord is another good tool. By moving these around the horse, you can make yourself seem quicker and bigger than him. Most lunge whips are too long, soft and bendy for effective use for groundwork but great for lunging later on. Some driving whips are perfect. Choose one that is well balanced and not whippy with a detachable tail, so that you can make your own. Jockey Club approved racing whips – again stiff not whippy – are perfect for ridden work and jumping or dressage whips with a good flap on the end are also ideal.

It is important to educate and 'gentle' your horse to your use of the tools – your stick and its 'tail' and your rope or lunge line. This is an early lesson in Effective Training (see p.68)

SOAK TIME

In all training sessions, it is vital to remember to offer 'soak time'. Soak time is necessary for both you and your horse; it is when work pauses and you both have a brief and quiet rest, allowing the 'penny to drop' and the lesson to sink in. It is one of the most important times for learning and, sadly, easily neglected in these days of hectic schedules. If you are doing groundwork, allow your horse to stand a few feet away from you. Leave him room to relax and lower his head and neck, he may lick and chew, which is him 'digesting a thought'. Stand quite still yourself with a soft middle and ask him to look at you, softly, with both eyes. If you are riding, let him stand 'at ease' on a completely loose rein and maybe rest a hindleg or let him walk on a loose rein; the important thing is to stay quiet and allow the horse to relax, think and digest his lesson.

AVOID INTENSIVE TRAINING

It is all too easy to spoil a horse's confidence and enthusiasm by asking more and more of him and keeping him under constant pressure for the whole lesson. This is one of the most frequent causes of sour horses. Sadly, especially in dressage training sessions, it is quite common to see horses shutting down after becoming angry and resistant having tried to understand and failed to gain release or appreciation until it is too late. Make sure your trainer knows you want to have regular breaks: trainers often feel under pressure to give you value for money, especially if they are on a tight schedule or you have travelled a long way. Occasionally, I also see horses shut down because they have lost interest through repeating tedious work with no stimulus or interaction – keep the work interesting.

Provide soak time at least every 15 minutes, preferably just after some good work, while you have a chat with the trainer or just rest yourself. In jumping training sessions it is fairly easy to provide soak time when the other horses are having their turn or the jumps are being altered, but with dressage training you need to remember to stop from time to time. A good horse trainer will always take great care not to over-face either the horse or the rider and ensure both receive adequate rest and reward, breaking the lesson for frequent explanation and discussion.

◁ Soak time is very important for learning to take place

◁ As her hands and legs are already occupied, Joanna is using a stick on the shoulder to help The Colt turn

Beginning Effective Training – using your body to train your horse

Say what you mean and mean what you say.

One of the most beautiful things about horses is their honesty. They reveal everything they are feeling through their body language. This means they also watch out for body language in every other horse, or human, that they come into contact with. A horse will interpret every movement and expression you make, whether you are aware you are making them or not. Horses are incapable of thinking one thing and expressing another, so they cannot understand that humans can do this, or that we don't always mean what we say. Rightly or wrongly, horses believe everything your body says, so avoid confusion, keep it clear and simple! We should try to follow their example and always try to say what we mean, and mean what we say with our bodies when we are with them.

All your training will be easier and more effective if you understand how your horse interprets your body language. Body language is a way of talking to your horse through your body movements. It is a vital ingredient in training a horse, but as with all training aids, you only need to use just as much as it takes to get what you want to happen, no more. Finding this delicate balance is the art of horsemanship, rather like having the correct ingredients in cooking or interpreting notes to make music. As with other forms of training, if the horse is not doing as he is being asked, the chances are it is because you are not asking correctly. Throughout your training and riding, you will need to keep on checking that your intention, body language and balance are working correctly.

READ THE SIGNS

If you were to walk into a room full of strangers, the chances are you would quickly be able to assess the attitude of people in it by reading their body language, and you will probably choose to approach the most welcoming-looking person. Remember this in your dealings with horses. When with a strange horse that is looking apprehensive, approach him non-threateningly and move him around reassuringly. Try not to be aggressive or defensive with horses, especially if they are making you nervous – they will read your fear – but move them around authoritatively (possibly from a distance) using confident body language to regain their respect. We always do several halt to walk-on transitions, in hand or ridden, before we begin work with any strange horse. Moving a horse's feet always earns respect.

• Body statements

Body statements are made through the way you align and hold your body and your intention; they warn the horse what to expect from you. Body statements are an important part of good leadership, whether you are riding or working in hand. They precede body language and signals (the aids) and it is their accuracy and effectiveness that help your horse to be successful in responding correctly to your aids. Keep it simple; avoid confusing him by giving conflicting information at the same time. Give one instruction at a time. He cannot slow and go all at once but he can slow then go. You can give the statements and signals in quick succession, depending on your skill level, dexterity and the speed with which you can change your body language.

• Body language

Body language is the way you use your body to communicate with your horse. For example, the most

⬆ Joanna uses her elbows to reinforce her sending away body language.

⬆ Without a line, Joanna draws The Colt to her by completely softening her centre and turning sideways, leading by a whisker

basic lesson to teach your horse is to respect your space. Imagine there is a bubble of at least 45cm (18in) all around you at all times, and he is not allowed into this bubble – that means no part of him. To achieve this respect for your space and to stay safe around horses in general, you need to be able to send a horse away from you, so the first body language to master is asking the horse to move away. If he comes too close, instantly become bigger and scarier than him and persevere until his feet move; the moment he moves, just as quickly drop your threat. If you get your timing right, he will not feel the need to continue the defence of flight – so he will simply move out of your space and then wait there. By keeping to the bubble rule you will gain his respect and he will want to stay with you politely at an acceptable distance. These are good manners, similar to people respecting each other's space.

The position and alignment of your hips and the core of your body – the area of your belly button, which is the centre of your energy – have a major influence on a horse. In simple terms, to send your

⬆ For rein back Daisy first uses a body statement to warn Gregory that she is going to ask for a step back, then she asks with body language, then signals her request. Gregory responds and gets a thank you

THE DIFFERENCE BETWEEN A BODY STATEMENT, BODY LANGUAGE AND A BODY SIGNAL OR AID

A *body statement* is made with your intention, stance and alignment and it forewarns the horse what to expect next; *body language* is how you use your body to make your request; and *body signals* are aids to tell the horse to move specific parts of his body.

So for example, imagine that you would like your horse to rein back from halt: the body statement, to warn the horse that you intend to ask him to step back is disallow the mental or physical energy to flow forward through your body and his; the body language is to deflate your centre and rock your pelvis back, rounding your back a little. The signal, if the horse fails to step back from the statement and language, is pressure on the mouth through the reins. Continue all the blocking pressures until he backs up a step, then release all pressures and reward with a 'yes'. Ridden in this way the horse will soon learn to respond to light signals or aids.

horse away your belly needs to be tight and your hip needs to push towards him. Drawing in is the opposite. You need to become soft in all your joints, exhale to deflate and soften your belly and whole body, and draw your hips sideways away from the horse's head, becoming smaller and keeping your eyes off his. Think of it as being like an inflatable and deflatable crab – and remember to check your posture as you approach your horse to catch him, for example. (For more information on these techniques and others, see the Glossary, pp.50–53.)

When using body language, your eyes can also communicate your intent. Although all horses hate being stared in the eye, they do not object to a gentle look – think of the lion they have been sharing oasis space with, as long as his eye remains soft the horses are safe, but the moment he fixes a horse with a focused predatorial stare, he intends to make a kill, so it's time for the horse to go. Remember you have a prey–predator relationship with your horse, too.

To find out how body language can work for you, try using jerky movements to sharpen up your horse's

◁ This is very obvious body language. Roger makes himself small to encourage a timid Whiskers nearer – a useful technique for catching a scared horse, although it is not usually necessary to be so exaggerated

◁ Roger rears up to send a rude Whiskers away. This is excellent for using in a crisis as it clearly states 'Do not run into me' and 'I can be bigger than you'

responses and soft flowing movements to calm him and draw him to you. I like my clients to practise walking through a flock of sheep without disturbing them, which is also useful for sneaking up on wildlife for a better view.

• Body signals

You can use body signals to back up body language. They are the physical aids and other signals that you use on the 'buttons' (see p.42) to ask your horse to do something. For example, one body signal to rein back is to put pressure on the horse's shoulder with your hand or stick. A horse has to interpret our body signals to find out what we want from him. We need to train him to have the confidence to make an attempt to guess what it is we are asking. We need to train ourselves to give clear and simple instructions that he can easily understand, and avoid confusing him. Humans and horses are brilliant at multi-tasking but keep your signals simple and use only one at a time!

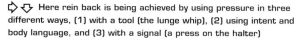 Here rein back is being achieved by using pressure in three different ways, (1) with a tool (the lunge whip), (2) using intent and body language, and (3) with a signal (a press on the halter)

Key training techniques – how to use pressure and release, advance and retreat, and positive and negative reinforcement

Pressure and release is a technique constantly used by horses and humans to control each other; it is very simple yet wonderfully effective. Pressure comes from a variety of sources: physical, environmental, social and emotional. For example, emotional pressure is someone asking you to do something, whether it is to pay the mortgage or weed the garden or, for a horse, to stand still to be plaited or jump the jumps. Physical pressure is someone pushing or prodding you to get you to do something. Release is achieved by yielding to, complying with or escaping from that pressure. Resistance to pressure occurs in many forms, including blocking, fighting, escaping and ignoring.

Horses instinctively push against pressure that they cannot escape by using flight or fight, so when training a horse, it is important to re-educate him to look for ways to overcome his defensive 'burst through' instincts and to yield instead, confident of finding immediate release when he gives the right response. The timing of releasing the pressure is vitally important as releasing at the right moment teaches him what is the right response and releasing at the wrong moment can teach the wrong response. This is why a structured plan is needed when training

⇧ Physical pressure produced by a tug on the halter. Charlie would prefer to break free from being held so tight

⇧ Environmental pressure in the form of cold water and boggy ground. Charlie would prefer not to be here

⇧ Social pressure created by Passion coming past Charlie. Roger maintains pressure until Charlie becomes gentle

⇧ Emotional pressure produced by the swinging rope. Charlie is fearful of it touching him. Rachel ensures it lands gently on his shoulders

horses, to educate the horse through a series of yields that become progressively more complicated. So, you don't begin with a half pass, you begin with walk to halt!

• Teaching pressure and release

To teach a horse the principles of pressure and release, apply pressure, matching like with like if there is resistance, until he moves or offers a try at the correct yield, whereupon instantly release the pressure to reward him (see also p.42). Whenever you feel he has tried hard for you have a little soak time together and give him a rub. Repeat the same exercise a couple more times and he will have learnt it. The pressure can come in the form of your intention, a glare, a touch, a nudge, a tap or a slap. Be consistently persistent and go through stages – ask politely, firmly, sharply, always in that order; ensure you are successful in your request before releasing pressure. Be sure your request is fair and avoid reverting to violence if your horse does not respond. Instead, do some revision and re-school his response to light pressure, politely (see p.62). It is never necessary or beneficial to become predatorial; this loses trust and respect.

Beware – don't confuse pressure and release with give and take – they are very different techniques. Give and take is when pressure is applied intermittently, usually to the rein; there is often no real response to this, so the horse is simply being trained to ignore the signal. This is very confusing training.

In your early stages of training and with a green horse, physical pressure is applied directly to the part of the horse that you want to move, but as his and your education progress he finds it easier to respond, so you can be more sensitive in your requests, and often just a look is enough pressure to have the horse yield for you. This way you can cultivate increasingly accurate communication between you and your horse up to a fantastically advanced level. Initially, training can take place on the ground and the aids (signals) should be progressively moved to the areas where the rider can easily give them with a hand or leg, such as the mouth or flank (see p.43).

⇨ Joanna politely asks The Colt to move his ribs over by pointing her stick behind the girth area (1); because The Colt does not respond she increases the pressure on the same spot, asking firmly (2); Again, there is no appropriate response so she asks sharply with a good tap. The Colt tries to move forward but finds Joanna is blocking his forward push so he finally gives a good sideways yield (3). Thank you. Good boy (4)

To help the horse learn, keep it very, very simple. Put pressure on when he is doing what you don't want, release instantly (take the pressure off) when he is doing what you do want. With good timing, your horse will learn to guess more quickly what you are asking him to do. Basically, you are making the right thing easy and the wrong thing hard. This sounds simple but it is not so simple to do well because it involves good timing, communication and decision-making (there is a reason why many good horsemen are also good with people). Keep practising – it's the only way to become skilled. Your horse will forgive an amazing number of mistakes!

Once your horse understands that he can successfully find release of pressure he will learn to seek the place of least resistance quickly and confidently, whatever the form of pressure. He will become confident and eager to try even harder to understand what you want him to do and, providing he is physically capable of doing so, will offer to do it to the best of his ability. Teaching this basic skill is how you can become a good leader and a good trainer; anyone can learn to do it, if they so desire, whether they are training horses, working in a profession or rearing a family.

LIGHT IS BRIGHT

Remember – always ask the horse to go off a light signal and if he ignores you ask again more firmly and if he ignores this, ask sharply. This is similar to riding when you use touch, press, kick, spur, stick until the right response is achieved. This way you will elicit ever lighter responses, as he understands the consequences of failing to respond to your polite ask is a firmer ask. Light is bright, heavy is dull, so too weak or too strong are equally as bad for both of you. Ask him to go from a whisper, not a shout!

• Advance and retreat

Advance and retreat is an effective technique for training or retraining a horse to accept difficult scenarios like clapping or umbrellas (see below). The principle is that you advance the difficulty of the scenario, whereupon the horse will probably brace ready for flight, but when the horse tries to accept it, usually shown by a softening in his body, you reward his try by instantly retreating the difficulty.

You can train a horse to accept an umbrella, for example, using advance and retreat. Begin with the umbrella furled up in the hand furthest from the horse, holding it soft and low. Raise it a little – the horse will brace, but as soon as he softens and accepts the new position, lower the umbrella again. Progress little by little.

• Noticing the try

During this work, when the horse 'tries' for you it is important to release. Tries can be very subtle, as small as a sigh, a soft look, a softening in the body or a step in the right direction; they can be as simple and small as not moving away from the rolled umbrella or the horse being brave enough to look at the water jump. Each try must be noticed, accepted and appreciated appropriately for his level of training. All that is needed is a small appreciative accepting gesture, and he will try even harder from then on. This is the way to start earning the horse's respect for your leadership. If you fail to notice or just fail to appreciate his efforts for you, he will stop trying or, even worse, he may start resisting.

Imagine you put great effort into a project for your boss, only to have your work go unnoticed and unappreciated; it would make you feel resentful, wouldn't it? Just a quick 'well-done old chap'-type rub or momentary release of pressure is enough. There is no need for lots of loud praising and patting, nor screeching to a halt and leaping off to reward him every time he tries for you – this type of reward usually

TIMING

With pressure and release work, timing is of the essence: releasing at the wrong moment or failing to release at the right moment will teach the wrong response. Thankfully, horses are patient and will tolerate endless mistakes, providing you don't blame or punish them for your own failings. Be sure you always allow your horse time to choose his response and to change his mind from a wrong response to a correct one. Keep practising, like any new skill it takes time to learn but will be worth it in the end. Have someone video you working and scrutinize the result to teach yourself. And beware – horses are naturally expert in their timing, and pressure and release techniques, so watch out that your horse is not training you!

◁ A horse learning to accept an umbrella through advance and retreat
1) Joanna touches the horse while holding the umbrella. He is a little braced
2) She advances pressure by degrees, first by stepping away and raising and slightly opening the umbrella
3) The horse tries hard to accept, so as soon as he softens he is rewarded by Joanna retreating the pressure – lowering and folding the umbrella
4) Advancing pressure again by opening the umbrella – the horse braces
5) As soon as he looks at the umbrella and softens Joanna rewards him by retreating again
6) He follows the umbrella with his ears pricked forward, indicating he is still a little worried. The work will continue progressively to increase his confidence with the umbrella

is too loud and too late. Noticing and accepting a try is a very powerful tool to use with horses and people. As you become more accomplished you will find you can use it to teach a horse to do anything you choose.

A very important part of developing your skill as a trainer is in deciding how much of a try to ask for and how much of a try to accept as worthy of a reward. As a horse progresses in his training you can ask for more of a try and only accept a higher level of effort.

⬆ Joanna acknowledges that stepping on the red cloth is asking a lot of The Colt (1). She notices that he has tried to please her and accepts his effort by rewarding him (2)

◁ Daisy asks Gregory to accept the pressure of a person clapping, she acknowledges that he has tried for her and rewards him by removing him from the pressure

WHO IS TRAINING WHOM?

I have been to many horse-training demonstrations where a single horse has taken just a few seconds to train an audience of hundreds of people never to clap or even to move in their seats, just through a few well-timed explosions. It works like magic! The audience moves, he leaps about, the audience freezes, he calms down. He has taken control; he has trained the audience not to move or he will explode. To reverse this process, the audience needs to continue to clap gently (advance), even if he explodes, until he tries to yield and calm down then the audience can stop clapping (retreat). Then gradually advance the difficulty by clapping louder and so on. This is teaching him that clapping is acceptable; he doesn't need to explode, and even if he does it won't stop the clapping; the clapping only stops when he is quiet. Now who is training whom?

Introduce clapping training at home and build up from a single person to a group to increase the pressure. Never use force to make the horse accept what you ask. Notice the partnership between Buddy and Rachel (1); he is licking and chewing, showing acceptance of her leadership. Gregory (2) is a little braced but progressing well

POSITIVE AND NEGATIVE REINFORCEMENT

Positive and negative reinforcement are used to educate the horse and cultivate his correct responses to the aids, of which there is more later (see pp.54–113). These terms are subject to much debate, confusion and misuse. Here is my interpretation of them. Positive reinforcement is when there is a pleasant outcome as a direct result of an action. Negative reinforcement is an unpleasant stimulus that will stop as the direct result of a good action. For example, when asking for a downward transition to halt, the pressure on the bit to ask a horse to stop is negative reinforcement and the release of the pressure the instant he halts is positive reinforcement. Therefore, the application of pressure is negative reinforcement and the release of pressure is positive reinforcement.

⬆ Using pressure on the mouth as negative reinforcement, JP asks Sid to halt. As soon as Sid complies JP releases the pressure on the bit, thereby giving Sid positive reinforcement as a reward for doing the right thing.

⇨ Using many buttons in quick succession, Joanna asks The Colt for a leg yield. He responds well and, despite the concentrated expression, her core is saying, 'Yes, well done'

Control buttons – fine-tuning your horse's responses

Buttons are places on a horse that you 'press' to ask him to make specific responses to aids or signals. First he needs to be taught the desired response and then you need to be consistent in using the same button to ask for same response – in this way you will gain good control of him. The spot where any button is located varies according to the level of training of the horse so, for instance, for a novice horse the 'hindquarters-move-over' button is near the hip, but for an advanced horse it is just behind the girth (see diagram opposite).

The use of pressure and release are the best way to teach him to respond lightly and confidently when these buttons are 'pressed'. Remember to use pressure in advancing stages, beginning with the lightest touch, to teach him to respond to lighter and lighter aids (see 'Light is Bright', p.38). Keep up the pressure in progressive degrees, asking politely, firmly and then sharply if necessary, until he gives the required response and then cease asking, release and reward.

The purpose of the exercises in section 2 (pp.54–113) is to educate and train your horse to be responsive to his buttons and your body aids to give you easier control. To do this efficiently you need to know which buttons to press, when and why. When you are teaching a horse, you need him to 'believe' that you really do mean what you say and that he really can trust you to be consistent, so plan your aids with careful thought. For example, always make sure the in-hand button for a particular response is as near as possible to the ridden button for the same response. This is one of the main reasons why Effective Training in-hand work is so beneficial in teaching the horse the desired responses in preparation for ridden work, as opposed to the traditional way of just lunging a horse around in side reins, which produces unfeeling pressures in places where neither a hand nor a leg can reach when riding.

Be careful not to rush or bore him during training sessions. Remember to give him plenty of brief breaks as 'soak time'. Most horses take about three half-hour sessions to get pretty good at responding to their buttons. The uneducated horse is a bit like a tank with the controls and gears far apart, but as he becomes more skilled he becomes more sophisticated, and eventually the buttons will become much closer together and he will progress to having the responsiveness and sensitivity of a Ferrari.

THE MAIN BUTTONS

There are eight main button locations. Select the appropriate one for the stage of training and whether you are working in hand or riding.

1: The 'shoulders-move-over' buttons are used to move or yield the shoulders, head and neck. They are found on the shoulder (1a), by the girth (1b) or on the neck (1c) (see Exercise 3, p.64).

2: The 'stop' buttons are used to block forward movement. They are found on the front of the shoulder (2a) or on the head (2b), nose (2c) or in the mouth (2d) (see Exercise 2, p.62).

3: The 'go' buttons are used to ask a horse to go forward. They are found just behind the girth (3a), on the back (3b) or in the space just behind the tail (3c). Remember to allow forward movement with the hands and body (see Exercise 6, pp.72 and 74).

4: The 'hindquarters-move-over' buttons are used to move the quarters over. They are found by the hip pin bone (4a) or along the flank (4b), depending on the stage of training (see Exercise 7, p.76).

5: The 'lateral flexion' buttons are used to ask the horse to bend and flex or yield in the neck, shoulder, ribs, pelvis. They are found on the neck (5a), shoulder (5b) and flank (5c) (see Exercise 10, p.84).

6: The 'direct flexion' buttons are used to ask the horse to flex at the poll and soften his jaw. They are found on the front of the head (6a) or in the mouth (6b) (see Exercise 15, p.100).

7: The 'move-over-sideways' buttons are a sequence lateral flexion (5c), go buttons (3a and 3b) and with shoulders over (1b) and hindquarters over (4b) as required.

8: For more advanced horses and riders the 'engage-this-hindleg' button (8) is found a little further back along the flank than the 'go' button and lower than the 'hindquarters-move-over' button and is used mostly for flying changes or extended trot or rein back.

Only ever use one aid or signal to request one move at a time, but when they are used in quick succession good lateral work can be more easily achieved. In the beginning, the buttons are positioned on the actual area of the horse you want to move, so you tap on the shoulder to move it over, for example. Later, the horse can be educated to move or yield from cultivated buttons so that a leg aid on just the right spot at the girth will mean move your shoulder over, please.

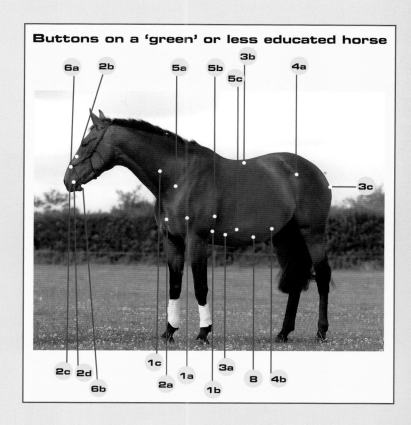

Buttons on a 'green' or less educated horse

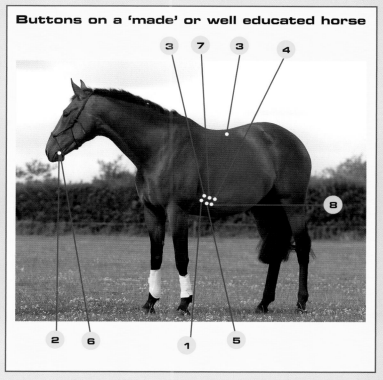

Buttons on a 'made' or well educated horse

YES AND NO GAME

The 'Yes No' game will give you a good idea of how your horse might feel when you are schooling him. In this game, one player (you) is sent out of earshot while the others (your friends) decide on a simple task for you to do, such as pick up a book off the floor. Like a horse, you cannot ask questions about what you are supposed to do and at first your friends can only use the word 'no' to get you to do what they want. Not easy is it? Imagine how despondent you feel after the sixth 'no' and the task remains undone. Next, imagine they can only use the word 'yes'. Again, this is not easy but each time you make a right move you feel elated and try harder. Eventually your friends manage to direct you to do the right thing.

Now imagine that they can use both 'yes' and 'no': you will feel elated by the 'yeses' but deflated by the 'nos'. If they use the controls thoughtfully it will be quite easy for you to guess what task it is they want you to do and you all feel a success. Now translate this into what you do with your horse and realize how easy it is for him to misinterpret what you are asking and how important it is for you to give him clear and accurate instructions, with plenty of yeses and not too many nos.

⬆ Be ready with the yes as soon as a horse gets it right. Konker is being told, no, pulling away is not the right reaction, then, yes, coming towards Joanna is correct. Note Joanna's neutral, unemotional body language – if she straightened up she would send him away. She follows his yield with a softer posture to reward his try (see page 148)

Clarity and understanding – honing your training skills

By now you will be beginning to realize how important your role is in how well and how quickly your horse learns. Your knowledge, experience and attitude all play a part in how he interacts with you. You do not need to be a brilliant rider to have a good working relationship with him. What is vital is to understand how he learns and what is important to him, and to be clear and consistent in the way you teach him.

⬆ Here Joanna is working through the yes no game with Jill. Jill tries to guess what Joanna is asking her to do. You can see her bracing against Joanna, who is blocking her forward movement – saying no – waiting for Jill to try to find the release from pressure by reining back. She steps back and gets a yes. Thank you

• Allowing and blocking – the horse's yes and no

A horse will try to find the place or line of least resistance so make it as easy as possible for him to guess what you want him to do by 'allowing' what is right and 'blocking' what is wrong. 'Allowing' can also be thought of as 'yes' and signals to the horse that he has done the right thing. 'Blocking' is 'no' and can be communicated through increased pressure or even a light smack (see 'Light is Bright', p.38). Use 'yes' much more often than 'no', this keeps the horse enthusiastic and trying to please you.

If the horse has managed to guess what you want him to do he will probably try to do it for you – they are very helpful creatures! Allow him to learn by his mistakes and successes and allow him to change his mind and receive the benefit, or suffer the consequences, of his actions. Never be tempted to ignore an unacceptable action from a horse, such as a rude nudge in the back. If you fail to react, he will interpret this as you accepting it and he will do it again. It is not that he is being intentionally rude but that you seemed to have said it was ok. If you do need to use a quick 'no', it is very important to administer it simultaneously with the mistake, quickly, painlessly and abruptly, with no follow-on persistence – hold no grudges or resentment. When they discipline each other, horses are quick to nip and quick to forgive. Punishment and pain are poor training tools and only breed resentment and fear.

⬆ As Joanna and The Colt negotiate the low jump before the water, he sees the water and thinks about evading through his right shoulder. Joanna says no and blocks his escape with her right hand and leg while still allowing him to come straight to the water. They drop into the water (note the well balanced rider position!) and then press on through with Joanna saying yes and allowing all the good things to flow

RIDING THE WAVE

Allowing and blocking are easy to understand when you think of a horse's energy as a wave flowing down a river. Your aids are the banks on either side and the dam gates at either end. Use them to direct the energy into the place that you want – called 'riding the wave' by Canadian horse trainer Chris Irwin. The more advanced your standards, the more discreet and complex the directing, or allowing and blocking, can become. In the beginning it is somewhat crude with the trainer blocking forward movement to stop the horse's flow and allowing him to come to a halt. Turns are made by blocking energy escaping out of one direction while allowing it to flow out of the other. Upward transitions are achieved by opening the front gates to allow energy forward while closing the gates behind to create forward movement. Downward transitions are made by blocking the flow of forward energy, while preventing energy escaping backwards.

For example, when riding an upward transition it is very important to soften the hand to allow the energy forward, while asking for impulsion from behind, then allowing this to flow. Later on in the training, things can become very sophisticated. For instance, by blocking all but a little flow out of the front gates while allowing some of the flow through the side bank and pushing lots of flow forward, you can produce a good half pass. This imagery is an easy way to explain some of the complexities of the rider's aids, keeping it simple for both horse and rider. As with all training good timing and consistency are everything and it is the release of pressure (see p.36) that tells the horse 'yes' that's what I wanted you to do, whereupon he will think 'Phew! I got something right'. At this point it is vital to give him a few moments of relaxation to understand the lesson and digest his thoughts – this is called 'soak time' (see p.31).

Praise and punishment – the importance of encouragement

Whenever you are training, be aware that there needs to be some benefit for the horse in what you ask him to do. He will ask you the question 'What's in it for me?' So have your answer ready! This is the backbone of this form of training because it is vital that there is always something good in it for him. Appreciation creates generosity and abuse leads to selfishness – even in horses (see also 'Timing', p.39.)

Be careful about the rewards you choose. Which do you prefer, an appreciative rub or a slap on the back? Horses love a stroke or good rub, but hate being patted – sometimes you see people pat their horse so hard it is more like a punishment. Always make praise a reward for the horse: a rest is much more appreciated than a polo mint, a good rub instead of a tidbit, a pick of grass instead of an immaculate stable; most important of all, well fitting saddlery instead of a new horsebox, or a good lifestyle instead of a new stable. You can always tell a real horseman by the way he rewards his horse and how often he allows him a brief break in his work.

The best way to teach a horse right from wrong is immediately to release pressure when he does the right thing. Praise is good but it can be too late and therefore it can be confusing for the horse to work

SELF-CONTROL

Part of becoming a good horseman is learning self-control. Consider this simple thought: if we can ask a horse not to toss his head when a fly lands on his chest in the middle of a dressage test then surely we can ask ourselves not to get angry when our zip jams on our overcoat. This is self-control, something we all struggle with, and it is even harder for a horse as he is so instinctively reactive, especially his flight or fight instincts. However, self-control is vital for good horsemanship. As your horse's personal trainer, it is important to learn to distance yourself from him and your emotions, so that you can concentrate on progressing his physical development in a practical way, rather than just focusing on your relationship together. Once you and your horse are the masters of your emotions then you can be masters of all. Good horsemen have endless self-control and patience, combined with tenacity, consistency and a little flair; they are formidable beings. A good horse will have these qualities in abundance, too. Your horse can help you to develop all these qualities in yourself.

⬇ Daisy's quick reactions put instant leg pressure on Flo for stopping and then immediately allowed her to go forward when she changed her mind. Daisy's hand allowed forward movement to flow well

out what he has done that is correct. For example, you might give him a quick rub in praise of a good transition, but unless your timing is instantaneous, he won't associate it with the transition. However, releasing the aid (pressure) instantly when he makes the transition, tells him very clearly he has done what you wanted. Sometimes it is not appropriate to give a rub or release, such as when you are in the middle of a dressage test in the main arena, then just thinking and feeling, 'Yes, well done mate' will soften your core muscles a fraction, which can tell him you are pleased.

• Punishment

The opposite of praise, punishment is when an unpleasant or painful action is given – not always at the same time as the horse made the 'mistake'. Never use punishment as a training tool as it is neither logical nor appropriate for horses. They are incapable of 'sinning' because they are incapable of intentionally doing wrong, therefore, they cannot understand punishment. They can understand making a mistake and getting hurt for a wrong decision, but only if that all happens instantly, 'now', in the present. Punishment is given retrospectively often long after the mistake and has no training benefit for horses: there is no point in shutting your horse in a darkened stable all day because he didn't do a good dressage test – how can he possibly connect the two actions? He does not have these levels of intelligence.

THROW YOUR HEART OVER THE FENCE

Joanna's mother had two favourite sayings: 'Throw your heart over the fence.' and 'Where you look, you land.' And they work! Riding is a complex art and emotions play a large role in how you perform. If are going to be the leader then you need to focus your energy over and beyond the obstacle (even if it is not a jump). Avoid allowing yourself or your horse to focus on its depths. Think positive and keep your chin up!

⬆ **Joanna and Peanuts throw their hearts over the fence**

Self-preservation – balance is essential for a horse's self-confidence

The major preservation skills a horse needs are balance, self-carriage and control of his feet. These are interdependent – you can't have one without the other – yet lack of balance is the most common fault seen in modern horses, and it leads to endless problems. The key to both balance and self-carriage is your horse's ability to distribute his weight evenly over all four feet.

Balance enables your horse to control himself physically. If he cannot stand in balance on his own four feet, he will find it far harder in walk, difficult in trot and impossible in canter. Balance is hugely important to horses. Without riders, they are naturally very well balanced: herds can gallop and turn as one, like shoals of fish or flocks of birds. It takes amazing levels of balance to be able to respond so instantly to minute changes around them. When their weight is evenly distributed over all four feet, horses feel confident because it gives them stability and athleticism to flee if necessary. Think about how you need to be balanced within yourself so you don't fall over when standing up. Now imagine what happens when you try to carry a heavy weight: it is more difficult for you to feel safe. This is exactly how it is for young recently backed horses, especially if you

ask them to negotiate obstacles too! Learning balance takes plenty of training and practise.

Self-carriage is also your horse's mental motivation and physical ability to carry himself and a rider without support or interference from the rider. It shows he is accepting his responsibility for balancing himself and his rider. Most of your horse's early training needs to focus on achieving self-carriage in all paces and all situations and if you succeed in this you will have a well-balanced horse. This repetitive training is often neglected, as it takes a lot of time and is not the most exciting part of bringing on young horses. Unfortunately, as a result, many horses learn to lean on the rider's hands because they have lost or never achieved self-carriage. If this leaning is not corrected, they will become desensitized and, therefore, 'hard' in the mouth. Roger and I spend a lot of time training horses to remain in self-carriage and be aware of where their feet are at all times. Think about the ballroom dancer who carries his weight in balance while performing difficult manoeuvres, and with a partner to consider too, this is what a horse needs to do when he is performing with you.

⇩ In New Zealand, Allan Dawson schools his show jumpers using natural hazards to develop their self-carriage, focus and confidence

⟨⟩ ⟨⟩ Using our little homemade hillock, we teach our horses to go powerfully up, lowering their heads and engaging their hindquarters, and come gently down. We ensure we stay light in the saddle to help the horses engage their backs

REFRAIN FROM USING GADGETS

To train a horse to 'find his feet' it is essential to allow him freedom to use his whole body to develop his balance, whether working in hand or being ridden. All gadgets interfere with this freedom and therefore prevent the progress to self-carriage. Your hands are far more sensitive and reactive than even the most sophisticated equipment. You have feel and intelligence – gadgets do not!

⟨ Roger rides up a creek on a horse at Jim Wright's Matahura Valley Farm in New Zealand. This station horse is sure-footed, bold and careful

Glossary – a reference guide to key terms

Adrenaline – see p.22.

Advance – This is when you increase the difficulty of what you are asking horse to do or accept (see also *retreat pressure*).

Aids – The signals made on the *buttons* that ask your horse to do something for you.

Allow – To allow energy to flow through (see also *block*).

Applying pressure – See *releasing pressure* and 'Levels of Pressure' box. You can apply pressure through your aids, your body, your tools, the situation, your expectation or your non-acceptance of the present offering.

Ask – A request for a try from you to the horse to perhaps walk on or gallop faster or jump higher or stop now. **Acknowledging an ask** – When you recognize that you have asked the horse to try for you.

Asking politely – Just as it sounds, not violent, not trying to force the horse (see also *asking firmly*, *asking sharply* in 'Levels of Pressure' box).

Backing – Having a horse learn to carry a human on his back. This is very unnatural for a horse as we are a predator, but very achievable. Most horses learn to like being ridden if backing is done well, it is often called 'starting'.

Banana shape – A soft lateral flexion through the whole horse.

Being big – Throwing your arms up and out, standing tall with a tight belly and feet wide apart (see also *being small*).

Being small – Crouching down low with a soft centre and eyes averted. Useful when you want to encourage very nervous horses to come close as it makes you less threatening (see also *being big* and *soft centre*, under *centre*).

Block – To disallow energy to pass (see also *allow*). Use in hand or ridden, with any part of the body, to prevent energy escaping in any direction other than the direction you want. (See also 'Riding the Wave', p.45.)

Body brace – Bracing belly muscles and spreading your feet with your knees bent ready to be strong enough to counteract a big pull on the rope from the horse that is trying to flee.

Body language – The way you or your horse express feelings or indicate requests with body movements. Actions such as aggression, friendliness, sending away, drawing, pushing and yielding are all body language.

Body signals – The aids and other signals that are used to ask a horse to do a particular thing, such as a touch to a button (see below) or a press of the leg to your horse's flank.

Body statement – Your or your horse's attitude and the way the body is aligned and held that informs others of the intention. Big, small, threatening, non-threatening, strong, weak are all body statements.

Bowing – see p.14.

Brace – How the horse instinctively resists your request to yield to pressure. Effective Training programmes and educates him to yield and soften to release pressure.

Breaking in – The initial training a horse undergoes when he starts working for people. Starting or gentling are better terms as this is the education that takes place.

Bump (accidentally on purpose) – This is when a bony elbow or wrist is put 'in the way' when a rude horse tries biting or invading your space.

Button – The place on which you give an *aid* to move certain parts of the horse (see also p.42).

SOME COMMON MOVEMENTS FROM A HORSE'S PERSPECTIVE

Come here – It is difficult for horses to understand you when you pull forward on the head because it is a very predatorial thing to do. Horses never do this to each other but lions do when they are dragging them down to kill. Yielding to pressure on the head needs to be taught and understood, especially before leading and tying up and particularly with foals. They need plenty of pressure and release training first (see p.36).

Go back or rein back – Rein back is also difficult because it is an emotional back down as well as physically quite difficult. The horse should step backwards softly lifting the feet up in diagonal pairs.

Move feet – This is significant to the horse because the one who moves the others feet is the leader. (For more about this see *moving his feet*.)

Flex poll or direct flexion – This is physically demanding and usually only done naturally in display, so maintaining it as a yield is very taxing for a horse.

Flex lateral or lateral flexion – This is also physically demanding but also very big emotionally. A rude horse will keep his ribs straight or pushed towards you and a respectful horse will flex his ribs away in a *banana shape*, even when working free, at liberty, providing your body alignment and language ask for this.

Push or be pushed (Chris Irwin) – This is the rule in the wild – so be sure you don't allow yourself to be pushed around. Push back! Work with courage and conviction whenever with horses.

Centre – This is your core or tummy button and it is considered the centre of your energy and your life force. By facing in the right direction (aligning) you can use it to project energy wherever you want. **Soft centre** is lightly rounded body with belly concave and smooth movements. Body language to use when you are being friendly. **Tight centre** is inhaling, breathing in, inflating yourself so you are full of air, stretching the centre of your body and standing tall. Body language to send away the horse. **Neutral** is normal posture, relaxed but upright, not giving off any specific signals.

Communication – Your horse uses body language and snorts and sighs to express himself (see p.14).

Core – see *centre*.

Deflate – Breathe out and soften centre (see also *centre* and *inflate*).

Disengage hindquarter – To move the horse's quarters away from behind his shoulders, thereby disempowering him by preventing engagement (see also *one rein stop*).

Draw – Encouraging the horse to come to you by drawing your core and hip away from him, moving in an arc backwards and sideways with soft centre (see also *send away* and *centre* and pp.32–35 on body language).

Driving – *Body language* to send horse on before you, either ahead of or beside you.

Emotions – Thoughts that influence *adrenaline*, *body language* and *impulsion*.

Energizing – Body language that encourages the giving of more energy.

Engagement – When the hindquarters lower and draw under the horse's belly to carry more of his weight (see also *impulsion*).

Fear – This is often shown as aggression, anger or anxiety in horses and people.

Free the feet – see *unlock stuck feet*.

Flexion – **Direct flexion** is when the horse relaxes in the jaw and flexes at the poll, bringing his face vertical yet keeping his poll as the highest point. **Overbending** is when the neck curls taking the horse's head towards his chest or knees. **Lateral flexion** is when the horse bends through his pelvis, ribs, shoulders and neck.

Focus – This is the ability to concentrate on one thing to the exclusion of all else, which is essential for predators, but dangerous for prey animals, because by doing so they could be caught by a 'tiger' sneaking up behind them. Horses, therefore, have to learn how to focus so they can perform as we want them to – jump a combination fence for example (see also *peripheral vision*).

Gentling – To have your horse remain gentle without bracing or fear. **Gentling to your tools** is educating your horse that your tools are not weapons. Asking the horse to stay 'gentle' while you are moving a stick, its string or your rope all over him, including around his legs (see p.68). Keep soft centre body language (see *centre*).

Go – A request to the horse to move his feet with more energy. Use mental and physical focus as well as the go button, and remember to *allow* the horse to go with your hands and body (see also *whoa*).

Goal setting – This is the skill of a good trainer and is essential to progress the horse (see p.56). It is better to progress one step at a time than in leaps and bounds, which risks a confidence crisis.

Going forward – Working forward with appropriate impulsion and emotional commitment.

Greeting – The way you approach your horse every time you meet him. Approach slowly with a *soft centre* and offer the back of your outstretched hand for him to smell, and allow him time to have a good old sniff because this will tell him lots of things he needs to know about you. Introduce yourself politely yet assertively, but don't barge into his space, nor allow him to barge into yours.

Halt – To stand still and square with weight balanced over all four feet and some energy held underneath a strong back and tight belly, waiting ready for the signal to move off (see also *whoa*).

Halter breaking/training – Teaching a horse to accept a halter and yield and respond to pressure on his head, which is very unnatural for them (see p.79).

Handling – The training a horse undergoes to be able to accept our strange world of farriers, vets, being groomed, wearing rugs and so on.

Impulsion – The power produced by the horse's hindquarters, his engine, to propel and lift him. This is an energy that comes from the heart. An offering from your horse, to be treasured (see also *engagement* and p.22).

Inflate – To draw in breath and make your centre tight and grow bigger (see also *being big*, *centre* and *deflate*).

Inside – The inside of the horse's bend, not necessarily the inside of the direction (see also *outside*).

Join up – Monty Roberts's speciality, and best left to the experts. Having the horse wanting to be with you because he has elected you as his leader. Physically the same as 'drawing' but far more complex as it usually follows sending away. Watch the horse's body language as frozen watchfulness (see p.15) can be mistaken for 'join up', when he chooses to be with you.

Lateral flexion – See *flexion*.

Leading by a whisker – This is a metaphor for drawing the horse to follow you just using your body language and then, once he is with you, pretending to lead him by a whisker, great training for learning body language, impresses your horse and your clients, creates a wonderful feeling of partnership and makes 'catching' your horse a doddle.

STICK SKILLS

Develop your stick handling skills by practising without a horse.

*A 1.2m (4ft) stick is an extension of your arm and the string an extension of that, so the stick and string just makes you 2.5m (8ft) bigger in every direction. (See p.28.)

*A 1.8–2m (6–8ft) stick is used with care to reinforce body language. It is a good tool for use when lunging but too long and bendy for close work.

*When using either of these long sticks there are 3 levels of pressure: tip level to ask politely, tip high to ask firmly, tip higher to ask sharply. Tip low is neutral.

*When riding, a non-whippy stick should be used and, like all your aids, applied in increasing levels of pressure from politely to firmly to sharply, always in that order to encourage lightness and only in support of the leg aids.

LEG AIDS

*The leg should be used in increasing levels of pressure to encourage lightness – a polite touch on the hair and if ignored a firm nudge and if ignored a sharp kick. Never use a leg more strongly than this. A (non-whippy) stick or spur should then be used to support the request. The leg should be used with a low heel and toe up to keep the calf muscles firm and accurate.

*The spur is an extension of the leg and should never be used on its own or as a prong to poke the horse. When correctly fitted horizontally just below the ankle it will only come into action as back up when a firm or sharp leg aid is used. It is important to ensure correct use of the leg with the heel kept down whenever riding in spurs. Correct and careful use of spurs improves the skilled rider's ability to control his horse's feet more accurately. For this reason, spurs are compulsory in advanced dressage tests.

Moving his feet – This is when you actively move a horse's feet around, ridden or in hand, to have his feet moving where you want, rather than let him move yours where he wants, such as when he is spooking. It is what herd leaders do too. They can move another horse's feet at any speed, in any direction, at any time – powerful stuff.

Napping – When the horse jibs and refuses to go forward or give impulsion (see p.22).

Neckstrap – Used to maintain the riders' balance, especially on young or unpredictable horses or when jumping. Can also be used to pull on to stop a horse.

No – When you *block* or put *pressure* on the horse for rudeness or an incorrect response. Must be followed by a *yes* as soon as he gets it right.

One rein stop – When only one rein is used to stop the horse. Once the horse has been taught this it is extremely effective because it disengages the hindquarters and thereby disempowers him (see also *disengage hindquarter*).

Outside – The outside of the horse's bend or flexion, not necessarily the direction he is moving in (see also *inside*).

Overbending – see *flexion*.

Over-facing – Asking too much too soon or too often, can result in *shutting down* or *napping*.

Peripheral vision – This is the inbuilt ability of all prey animals (including horses) to be able to see a wide area around them. As predators, this is not natural to us, we have to learn how to do this to be able to work better with our horses (see also *focus*).

Praise – To tell a horse how well he has done, often after the event, so it is of no training value. Not to be confused with *reward* or release.

Pressure – For a horse, physical pressure is your aids and body language, environmental pressure is the world around him and particular situations he finds himself in, emotional pressure is his emotional state, while social pressure comes from interaction with his peers (see also 'Levels of Pressure' box, p.51).

Rear – Body language whereby you instantly grow big and tall, extending your arms as high and wide as you can. (See also *being big* and *being small*.) Horses can do this, too.

Releasing pressure – Is just that, whether it is a physical, mental, emotional or social. The removal of pressure means, 'Yes, that's right', whether you intended it to mean that or not, so timing is crucial to good schooling.

Resistance – When an animal or person braces against the push of another animal or person, either mentally or physically.

Retreat pressure – Backing off or retreating to say, for example, 'Thanks for trying'. It can also be a wise move if you have inadvertently over-faced a horse (see also *releasing pressure*).

Reward – Release of pressure and a mane rub are usually all that is needed to make a horse feel appreciated. For good training, the timing needs to be precise, the instant the horse gives the correct response, even if it means just thinking 'Yes, thanks'. Rewarding after the event has no training purpose but does no harm unless it is given when horse is doing something undesirable (see *praise*).

Riding the wave – see p.45.

Send away – Push hip towards horse and maybe *rear* a little to send all or part of him away from you. (See also *draw*.)

Shutting down – When a horse closes down and ceases to communicate, usually due to discomfort or over-facing.

Slide – When a horse continues in a movement as his impetus carries him along. It is allowed in the early stages of learning something new.

Soak time – see p.31.

Stable manners – How well the horse behaves in his stable – this will depend on how well you have trained him and how gentle he has become, even when confined in a box.

Stop – To stop the horse's feet moving (see also *halt* and *whoa*). Also used to describe a horse refusing a jump.

Tools – Equipment used to make your communication with your horse more effective (see also *body signals* and p.28).

Trainer – The person who is with the horse is his trainer at that moment – a famous saying of the old masters.

Trust – The confidence in the care, consideration and predictable responses of another that creates a respectful and trusting bond between two or more beings.

Try – A try is when a horse makes a conscious effort to give physically, mentally or emotionally for his trainer. **Noticing a try** is seeing or feeling the instant of giving, in any way in response to your ask. **Accepting a try** is when the trainer decides to accept the horse's attempt, even if it is only partial or not perfect (see also *ask*). **Acknowledging a try** is acknowledging that the horse has tried for you. **Appreciating a try** is showing appreciation for effort. Failing to notice, squandering effort or ignoring a try will seriously damage your relationship and the horse's enthusiasm.

Unlock stuck feet – To 'unlock stuck feet' or 'free the feet' are expressions for anything done to help the horse realize he can still move his feet when he gets stuck. One common manoeuvre is when the trainer moves out to the side while maintaining pressure on the head to unbalance the horse and get his feet moving again.

Whoa – A request from you to the horse to ask him to slow down or stop his feet. Make this clear to the horse by continuing the pressure on his head until he slows his feet and only then release, otherwise you're just pulling at his head (see also *go* and *halt*).

Yes – Allowing and an inner softening of your core muscles and joy in your soul that tells the horse he has got it right (see also *no*).

Yield – Softening physically, mentally or emotionally, the withdrawal of resistance. Also applies when you yield to a horse in acceptance of his yield to you.

ROPE WORK

Develop your rope skills without a horse first. Good practice makes perfect with rope work.

Bump with the rope – Swinging the coils of rope or line to touch the horse and give him a signal. Should also be used through the levels of pressure.

Flick of the rope – Using the end or the belly of the rope to reinforce your aids. It can be used when increasing pressure levels.

Send a loop down the rope – You flick a loop along the rope to bump the horse on whatever part you require, nose, shoulder, flank, depending on your level of skill. Before using it with your horse, make sure you can get it right by practising. Do this by tying a rope to an old kitchen chair and flicking a loop down to it, trying to get the chair to move where you want.

Twirl the rope – This is very aggressive as with a twirling mane or tail. It is best avoided unless you need to stress to a horse that you really do mean business.

DEVELOPING YOUR OWN FEARLESS HORSE

20 exercises to help you master Effective Training techniques and strategies

This section consists of a series of exercises that together make up our Effective Training approach. Their main purpose is to educate the horse to respond to the different buttons (see p.42) and develop their use from basic novice aids to subtle advanced ones. This will eventually produce a horse that is easily controlled and can accurately interpret your aids.

To begin with the ideas may seem complex and the exercises might take ages to do, but as you and your horse master each one, you will simply need to revise them as and when necessary. You don't have to do all of the exercises every day. They are in a logically progressive order to be gradually worked through from 1–20, and once they are established in your horse, the foundations should remain in place forever. You should also find that any current difficulties you have with your horse will disappear as you progress through them.

Effective Training is suitable for horses, ponies and people of all ages and abilities. The work helps horses and ponies become strong and supple and stay sound and safe, even into their dotage. Youngsters benefit hugely from the in-hand work, as do children's ponies if their little riders are at school. There are no specific 'breaking in' or 'starting' exercises as all Effective Training exercises can be used to prepare a youngster for backing when the time comes.

INTENTION AND BODY LANGUAGE

Thoughout this book much importance is placed on your alignment and body language, and your horse's ability to interpret everything you say and believe your every 'word' or expression, whether intentional or not. If your intention is right and you are clear in your mind what you want to do, your body language will be right too, because it is the intention that creates the body language. Then all you need to remember is which bit you want to send away and which bit you want to draw nearer to you, or which to quicken and which to slow. Get your intention right and your horse will understand, believe and respect you, and do as you ask.

⬆ Blocking Passion and drawing The Colt

⬆ Roger uses pressure and release techniques to good effect when riding a well schooled show jumper ...

⇧ ... and obeys the countryside law without dismounting as he crosses farmland in New Zealand

How to approach the exercises

Each exercise is set out in the same way so that they are easy to understand and follow. Most can be done both in hand or under saddle and, to help you do them well, we have included any pitfalls you might come across as you learn. Under 'goal' you can read how far you will ultimately be able to go, but you decide how far you want to progress each time you do the exercise. (Use the chart on p.43 as a reference and reminder of where the buttons are.)

Although these exercises are great add-on skills to what you already know and do with your horse, you may find your family or friends are surprisingly unsupportive when you start to try them. Not everyone welcomes change because it 'rocks the boat', so don't get disheartened by lack of enthusiasm from others. Once they see what you are achieving, and how much more easily you can control your horse, they will soon change their minds.

Try not to be overwhelmed by the task ahead, either. The good thing about the future is that it comes just one day at a time. Remember this and try to understand and improve a little each day – don't attempt to change everything all at once. And, continue enjoying your horse as usual – riding and competing – while you work through the exercises.

⬆ The Colt – from a young thug...to a gentleman

⬆ Friendly critics can become encouraging supporters

Setting goals

A good boss will ensure that his junior colleagues are well educated and equipped to cope with anything that comes their way. The same applies to you and your horse. Whatever you want him to do, it is your responsibility to make sure that both you and he are adequately prepared, both physically and mentally – this is part of good goal setting. It is through the setting of the goal (or the levels of difficulty of the

work, or the speed of progress) that you can make or break a horse – too big a goal and you will over-face him, too small and he will become bored and dull.

Work progressively through the skills, gradually stretching the boundaries of your comfort zones. And remember, it is just as ok for you to make a mistake as it is for your horse to make one; when you are learning, be a bit lenient with each other! Remember to frequently ask yourself: 'What's in it for whom?', and be sure your horse gains some benefit for his efforts.

Keep sessions short and sweet. It is far better to stop too soon than to regret continuing for too long. This work is very demanding of horse and human, both mentally and emotionally, and in the early sessions just 10 minutes is enough. It is not necessary to complete a task in one session – providing you are always heading along in the direction of your goal, all is well. A few minutes every time you are together is infinitely preferable to long sessions, although if you have a big issue to overcome, it may take some hours to resolve the situation. To make sure you don't overdo it, please reread 'Listen to Your Horse' (p.14) before you begin, and keep it in mind whenever you are with your horse and whatever you are doing with him.

Is it working? – assessing your progress
Good, thorough training and development of responses to the 'buttons' should give you the ability to control a horse's feet, at any speed, in any direction, and at any time. If you can do this, as well as control your horse's emotions, then he is accepting your leadership and you know your training has been good. It is development of this training that will produce the fearless horse. If a request is met with an incorrect response or thoughtless reaction, then more good training is needed. Remember that it's always up to you to show your horse what it is that you would like him to do for you. He can only guess from your body signals and pressure and release work, so be fair and clear, and allow him to digest his learning with frequent soak times.

REMEMBER TO REWARD THE TRY

In learning anything new, it is the success of the first stumbling attempts that encourages more effort. When you first ask for a new move from your horse, the slightest effort must be rewarded, to show him 'Yes – that's right'. Later as that move becomes familiar that same level of effort need not be so significantly rewarded, this is how you make progress (see 'Noticing the Try', p.39).

Often progress is made in leaps and bounds with the occasional setback. Don't worry about setbacks; they are almost inevitable. See each one as an opportunity to revise that scenario, consolidating the foundations. It is never a crisis – just a learning opportunity. (For more information on overcoming specific difficulties, see pp.114–149.)

When training it is a really good idea to judge your progress by asking yourself questions. For example: can my horse stand loose while I spray fly repellent on him? Can my horse trot through these poles? Can my horse perform travers? Can my horse jump that ditch? '*Can* my horse' means that the emphasis is on your prior training, while '*will* my horse' or '*can I make* my horse' puts the emphasis on something you force him to do. In each of the following exercises I have suggested questions you can ask yourself to find out whether your horse has understood the lesson and benefited from it.

⇩ Can Highland Lad stand calmly and lift up one foot while someone else works on his other side? Yes! Great progress for a horse that is worried at competitions

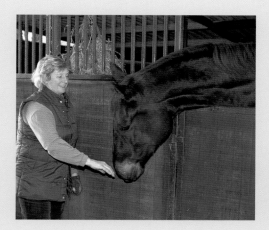

⇧ Offer the horse the back of your outstretched hand to sniff in greeting

BEFORE YOU BEGIN...
When you approach any horse reach out to offer the back of your hand in greeting, to be sniffed, just as horses reach out their noses to greet each other.

EQUIPMENT AND TOOLS CHART

Use this table to help you select appropriate equipment and tools for working with your horse. Remember it is your consistency, timing and expressing your intention through clear body language, as well as interpreting his, that will develop a trusting and respectful working partnership between you and your horse. Equipment and tools are for use just as an extension of that body language, to help you seem quicker or bigger, not for use as a weapon! Cultivate your skills without a horse first.

✓ Equipment for use both in hand or ridden
✓ Equipment to be used in hand *only*

EXERCISE	1	2	3	4	5	6a	6b	6c	7	8	9	10	11	12	13	14	15	16	17	18	19	20
hat, gloves, boots	✓	✓	✓	✓	✓	✓	✓	✓	✓	✓	✓	✓	✓	✓	✓	✓	✓	✓	✓	✓	✓	✓
80cm (2½ft) stick	✓	✓	✓	✓	✓	✓	✓	✓	✓	✓	✓	✓	✓	✓	✓	✓	✓	✓	✓	✓	✓	✓
1.2m (4ft) stick	✓	✓	✓	✓	✓	✓	✓	✓	✓	✓	✓	✓	✓	✓	✓	✓	✓	✓	✓	✓	✓	✓
1.2m (4ft) stick with 1.8m (6ft) string/tail				✓	✓	✓	✓	✓	✓	✓	✓	✓	✓	✓	✓	✓	✓	✓	✓	✓	✓	✓
Lunging whip or 1.8m (6ft) stick with tail				✓	✓	✓	✓	✓	✓	✓	✓	✓	✓	✓	✓	✓	✓	✓	✓	✓	✓	✓
2.5m (8ft) rope	✓	✓	✓	✓	✓	✓	✓	✓	✓	✓	✓	✓	✓	✓	✓	✓	✓	✓	✓	✓	✓	✓
5m (14ft) rope	✓	✓	✓	✓	✓	✓	✓	✓	✓	✓	✓	✓	✓	✓	✓	✓	✓	✓	✓	✓	✓	✓
6m (20ft) lunge line	✓	✓	✓	✓	✓	✓	✓	✓	✓	✓	✓	✓	✓	✓	✓	✓	✓	✓	✓	✓	✓	✓
Knotted halter	✓	✓	✓	✓	✓	✓	✓	✓	✓	✓	✓	✓	✓	✓	✓	✓	✓	✓	✓	✓	✓	✓
Bridle*	✓	✓	✓	✓	✓	✓	✓	✓	✓	✓	✓	✓	✓	✓	✓	✓	✓	✓	✓	✓	✓	✓
Dually	✓	✓	✓	✓	✓	✓	✓	✓	✓	✓	✓	✓	✓	✓	✓	✓	✓	✓	✓	✓	✓	✓
Cavesson	✓	✓	✓	✓	✓	✓	✓	✓	✓	✓	✓	✓	✓	✓	✓	✓	✓	✓	✓	✓	✓	✓
People and special equipment																				✓	✓	✓

*A bit ring link should be used whenever working a horse in a bridle in hand. It is just a simple short strap to prevent the bit rings from inverting and turning forwards when the horse tosses his head or the rein is inadvertently pulled forward. Attached to both bit rings and passing behind the horses chin, a pelham 'D' is ideal, or two light clips joined with a bit of boot lace.

The exercises

⌂ Be innovative – make use of safe, everyday equipment to assist you. For example, pieces of heavy tarpaulin can be makeshift ditches or water, and a can filled with pebbles and shaken simulates the sound of clapping

NOSEBANDS

Skilled horsemen do not need tight nosebands as they school their horses to remain soft throughout, especially in the mouth and jaw, truly on the bit. Sadly, nowadays, tight nosebands are frequently used to mask resistance in the horse, which shows in his mouth. This is especially common in competition in an attempt to fool the judges. However, comfortable fitted nosebands are extremely useful for helping uneducated horses to learn not to evade the bit by opening their mouth. They also help horses remain easier to control in fast work such as on the gallops, when hunting, going across country or show jumping. Fit nosebands with care, and be aware of the discomfort caued by a clamped shut jaw.

Exercise 1: Developing respect for your personal space

Why? This exercise introduces you and the horse to the effectiveness of pressure and release. Your task is to use the pressure of your body language to create an imaginary safety barrier between you and the horse and for the horse to learn to understand that sending body language means he should move out of your space, and once he does so the pressure is released (the sending body language stops). This ensures that you stay safe and your horse learns to be polite and respectful of your personal space. Use this exercise whenever and wherever you are near any pushy horse whether in the stable, field or horse transporter. It is especially useful with strange horses to avoid you getting bumped into or a squashed foot. As the senior partner you can politely move into the horse's space, but he should never move into yours – never, even if scared, over-excited or angry, should he forget his manners. Begin as you intend to continue – with mutual respect. You need to immediately establish yourself in the lead role by moving his feet.

How? Begin by creating an imaginary 45cm (18in) bubble all around you in every direction, especially around your head (see p.32). Make sure your lead rope is long enough to allow this and that you are not inadvertently pulling the horse into your space. Politely but convincingly ask him to move away a step by using sending body language – stand very upright and point your tight centre at his chest while standing in front of him and pushing on his nose with your hand or backwards on the halter or tapping his chest. Reward him by immediately releasing the pressure when he steps back. If he doesn't move for your polite ask, work up through a firm ask to a sharp ask, using the end of your rope to flick on his chest or even stamping your feet to reinforce your request if necessary. Any time he moves too close, quickly use blocking body language and point your centre at the part that is too close to push it away; swing your rope, arm or stick too, if necessary. If he puts his nose or head too close let him 'accidentally on purpose' bump himself on your firmed elbow, wrist or head (only if you have a hard hat on). This ensures that he finds the consequences of moving too close to you uncomfortable – this is being educationally assertive. Reward him with a rub as soon as he responds to the 'bump'. Make sure your body language doesn't encourage him to walk all over you and that you don't let him push at you to make you move your feet. Repeat the pressure and release process a few times until he waits politely at a respectful distance and you can then reach out and give him a good thank-you rub. Beware of accidentally tugging him back into your space as you do this.

HOW SHOULD IT FEEL? As though the horse waits near you politely and respectfully, never pushing at you.

GOAL: To have a polite and friendly horse that confidently respects your space and does not tread all over you or knock you about, even in a crisis.

PITFALLS: Avoid striking out at him or asking roughly or violently: that is rude, aggressive and predatorial, all the things we are trying to teach him that we are not. Be very fair and set a good example. Ensure he

▷ Can your horse be gentle and affectionate without ever invading your space?

⬆ The Colt tries to barge out of the door. Joanna blocks him and sends him back – Joanna should be wearing a hard hat!

⬆ Now, he waits much more politely for the door to be opened and to be invited out

moves his feet away as well as his head, otherwise he may just take his head to the side and bump you with his shoulder. Remember your manners too – use plenty of pleases and thank yous.

CAN YOUR HORSE... refrain from ever invading your space yet be gentle and affectionate, enjoying you rubbing him when you choose to but never trying to rub on you?

⬆ Roger trains Whiskers to move out of his space by sending a loop down the rope towards her – the swing of belly of the rope is the signal to move back

⬆ Even when schooling or competing never allow the horse to push into you. Konker is fearful of the jump behind him, but still moves his feet when asked

Exercise 2: Cultivating the stop and rein back buttons

Why? To introduce and cultivate the stop buttons, which can be on the nose if you are using a halter, in the mouth if you are using a bridle, or on the chest if you are working the horse loose. You want your horse to respect you, and to do this you need to be able to stop him from pushing through you, which you do by blocking his forward movement whenever you want to. For him this is hard because all his energy naturally flows forward from his rear end engine (see 'Riding the Wave', p.45), unless he learns to rebalance and engage his hindquarters. Your ultimate goal is to gain control of all his feet, which he will only *allow* if he feels confident in entrusting you with his whole body and can only *achieve* if he is balanced over all four feet and knows his buttons. Use the techniques described here whenever any horse pushes at you, as it is a very rude and disrespectful thing to do to you.

How? IN HAND: With the horse walking forward begin to apply pressure to the stop button on his head to ask him to slow his feet down, then turn to face him and ask him to stop. Block any forward movement with your hand, on his halter or reins, applying pressure and possibly tapping your stick or rope on his chest stop button. Repeat the walk to halt until he has understood that to release the pressure on the stop button he needs to stop his feet.

Once he is standing balanced and relaxed on a loose rein, ask him to back up by applying pressure to the stop button at the halt, which turns it into a rein back button. Begin with the horse at arm's length straight in front of and facing you and be ready to block his forward movement by standing extra tall and square facing him, pointing your centre at his chest. Place your hand on the back of his headcollar or bridle and apply pressure to the stop button, pushing backwards towards his hind feet to ask him to back up a step. Make sure your arms are held very

straight with the elbow locked. Wait, just keeping the pressure constant on the button until he gives you the right response. The moment he moves backwards, even an inch, release the pressure and ask him to stay still there balanced over his own feet while you both pause for a little soak time, then repeat, repeat, repeat until he backs up easily as soon as you press the stop button, one step at a time, slowly, softly and straight. Alternatively, you can apply pressure to his chest stop button (remember to go through the levels of pressure, p.51). Persist until he moves back.

RIDDEN: Cultivate the stop and rein back button in hand before you introduce it ridden. At walk use a blocking forward movement body statement by breathing right out, tightening your thighs and staying tall and light in the seat. If he fails to answer your body statement then apply a steady pressure on the stop button with the reins until he stops still, then release the pressure immediately to establish the halt. If you want to continue into rein back maintain the pressure on the

3

⬆ ◁ Roger blocks Whisker's forward movement and waits for her to work out what he is asking for. She finds the release from pressure by correctly stepping backwards. Well done. Now do it again. Well done, thanks!

See page 33 for ridden rein back and use of body language

stop button while adopting the same body statement and also rocking your pelvis backwards to encourage him to lift his withers and come backwards with you and drawing your lower leg back to ask his hindlegs to engage. Release pressure and reward him the instant he moves back at all and continue to progress as for the in-hand work. It is important that he remains soft and round in his body with a low head, and that his feet lift athletically in diagonal pairs (see also p.33).

HOW SHOULD IT FEEL? You press the back-up button, he moves, you release, thank you – step-by-step. The feeling should not be forced or hurried, but a backward yield with a soft body, not braced against the hand. Look for a two-time movement, with the horse's legs moving in diagonal pairs.

GOAL: To be able to ask your horse to come forward a few steps and back a few steps, in response to your aids, like a dance, forwards and back, forwards and back, elegantly and softly with a rounded back and a low head, yielding to and fro. Eventually you will be able to stop, slow or back up his feet whenever you want to, in hand or ridden.

PITFALLS: Beware of him dropping his back and sticking his chest out and just raising his head to try to release the pressure, and not actually moving his feet. If his knees get locked and his feet stuck into the ground, yield him over to one side first to free them up. If you increase the pressure on his head he may rear as he will feel trapped and unable to move. Remember he needs to learn how to move or slow his feet to release pressure on his stop button, before he can manage to rein back. Also be sure to ask for only one diagonal step at a time until he is competent, so that he doesn't learn to rush backwards, and use more yeses than nos, to retain his enthusiasm.

CAN YOUR HORSE… stop quickly and easily whenever you press that stop button?

LONG–TERM BENEFITS: This exercise is excellent preparation for achieving a responsive mouth and a quality rein back, with your horse softly lifting each diagonal pair of feet in good rhythm and with a good outline, for just the number of steps requested and in a straight line. In jumping he will find it easier and quicker to rebalance after the fence and engage in his hindquarters. The better a horse is at rein back, the better his forward work will be.

Exercise 3: Teaching the shoulder-move-over button

Why? One of the most important lessons a horse needs to learn is that you can move his feet in any direction at any time and that he can find release from your pressure on the button by moving his feet in the required direction. Moving the shoulders is very important because whenever he loses his balance, a horse will drop onto a shoulder. Also it is usually the shoulder that is used by a horse to gain freedom, to escape by knocking you over or to drop to throw you off. He will use his shoulder to push, threaten, resist or bully, both when in hand or ridden; but when he is being respectful he will work with an upright shoulder. This exercise asks a lot of him as his shoulder is the heaviest part of his body to move around.

How? IN HAND: Begin by standing on the left side of the horse, facing towards him, with your left hand on the side of the halter or bridle to help move his head around or block any unwanted forward movement. Place your right hand on his shoulder and ask him to move the shoulder and his feet just one step away from you by putting pressure on his shoulder-move-over button – touching, tapping or smacking a spot on the side of his shoulder with your stick or the end of the lead rope. Adopt sending body language and point your centre at his shoulder too. Remember to allow enough rope to let him move away from you. Release all pressure the instant he moves. Accept his try by standing soft and quiet by him, offering him a loose rope and maybe reach out and give him a quiet rub.

After a few moments of pause, ask for another step by applying pressure on the button as before and releasing the moment he tries for you. Make sure the front end of the horse is moving around the back end – eventually you want to have the front legs crossing over in front of each other – as it would when you are turning a horse when 'trotting up' or for a vet inspection. Repeat this 4 or 5 times and then allow soak time of a few minutes for him to digest his lesson, which is: by moving his feet in the required direction in response to your ask he can find release of pressure, and this entails him having to put effort into rebalancing himself, for which he will be rewarded. Have a soak and allow him enough space and time to bow his head low and lick and chew if he

⬆ Roger and Whiskers make a good start at moving the shoulders

wants to (see box below). Repeat the exercise on the other side.

To cultivate the button for ridden work, during your in-hand training progressively move the spot where you apply pressure back from the shoulder via the elbow to the girth area until he will move his shoulders from an ask by the girth.

RIDDEN: The same principles apply during riding but you will be asking with the reins acting on the mouth and with the outside leg on the shoulder-move-over button beside the girth and maybe a slappy stick on the outside shoulder-move-over-button. The leg on the inside of the turn allows him to move over but, assisted by the hands, prevents any unrequired movement from his quarters or shoulders.

HOW SHOULD IT FEEL? Awkward at first, because the shoulder is a large area to move. Take your time and feel him move his shoulder over and away in response to your pressure and proceed unhurriedly

A SIGNIFICANT MOMENT

The first move of a horse from pressure in this way can represent a huge change in the relationship between you and him, especially if this is the first time anyone has shown him good leadership in a way he can understand – in his own language of pressure and release. Most horses will be very impressed and will demonstrate this through yawning, licking and chewing. Allow them time and space to do this.

⬆ Whiskers is trying hard but her hind feet are getting stuck

⬆ Another step then, well-tried, thank you, have some soak time

– pressure, move, release, thanks, pressure, move, release, thanks. Keep the learning slow but sure.

GOAL: Over a few sessions, build up to a quarter and then a half and eventually a full turn. Although it may be rather crude at this early stage, you should still be looking for a soft athletic movement from the horse. Eventually, you will want him to cross his nearest front leg in front of the other one and pirouette a little on his hindlegs – lifting his hind feet up and down marking

time in a tiny circle rather than just planting them down and swivelling them into the ground. Build on the basic response to the button over the coming sessions until he can do a full walk pirouette in hand or ridden with quality and ease.

PITFALLS: Be prepared to block forward movement with your hand strongly on the back of the halter or bridle, it is important he doesn't walk forward or backward when turning. Be careful not to rush – the basic movement may take 10 minutes to achieve, especially if you are both learning; have a think before you begin and be sure you are organized and know in your own head exactly what you want him to do. You want him to reorganize his balance and yield his front feet away from you. You don't want him spinning on his middle around you like a bottle on its side or pushing over the top of you. Be sure to use more yeses than nos.

CAN YOUR HORSE… politely move his forehand around his quarters without pushing against your hand, both ways?

LONG-TERM BENEFITS: This exercise helps horses with lifting the forehand and positioning the shoulder, turn on the haunches and pirouettes. In jumping it improves control of shoulders to hold a straight line or make turns.

◁ A turn on the haunches with the hindleg active but almost marking time. Unfortunately, Gregory has toppled onto his shoulder slightly. The movement is similar to half pass on the circle

Exercise 4: Staying gentle with people

Why? Whatever you do with him, you need your horse to accept you moving all around him. This is known as 'gentling' and it can be used in any training session, and even whenever you meet a new horse. It will help build up his trust in humans (natural predators). To a horse, people are unpredictable and, sadly, these days, most know nothing about how to approach livestock or horses. Your horse has to survive in a world full of them so he needs your help to learn to overcome his natural apprehension. He also needs to learn to interpret our body language so he can tell the difference between an arm flung in friendship and an arm flung with intent to harm, and respond appropriately to ensure his and your safety. Gentling is also the pre-training for first bath, first rugs, first tack, fly spray, clipping, so it is a vital part of his repertoire and absolutely essential before riding.

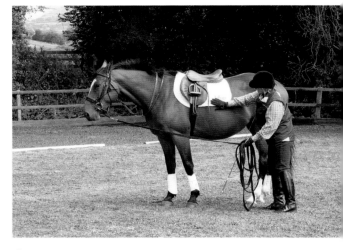

⇧ Joanna asks Jill to stay gentle while she touches her all over

⇩ Daisy asks Flo to accept a lot of human movement and touch as she is mounted

How? IN HAND: Adopt soft and non-driving neutral body language and have soft belly muscles so your centre is not pointed anywhere. Ask the horse to stand still (see previous exercises) and begin by just stroking him in a non-driving manner on his shoulder and progress inch by inch until you can touch him all over his body. If you reach an area he is worried about, ask him to accept your hand pressed consistently near it and when he shows acceptance by softening his body or sighing, only then withdraw your hand. Don't avoid the area nor allow him to tell you to take your hand away; you should be training him but he will try hard to train you – remember the demo horse (see 'Who is Training Whom?', p.40). If you meet a lot of resistance, try moving his feet (see p.52) to reassert yourself as his trustworthy leader. Continue carefully using these advance and retreat techniques until you are satisfied that the horse is gentle enough to move on to the next area. Progressively build up the speed and weight of your touch but always with non-sending neutral body language. You don't have to get him perfectly confident in every area of his body on the first session. For riding, his back, belly, head and neck are important areas; for lunging, he needs to be gentle with you moving around him quite fast, especially around behind him, and he will need to be gentle with a whip and lunge line moving around him, including his legs and under his tail, too.

RIDDEN: Applying the same principles, touch him carefully with your stick and hand everywhere you can reach; try rubbing him all over and eventually patting him all over too.

⬆ Whisky learns that some riders might be clumsy when on board

HOW SHOULD IT FEEL? As though the horse trusts you; as if he no longer thinks of you as a threat, but as a partner, however fast you move.

GOAL: To be able to touch him anywhere at any speed and at any time. Also to be able to spray, bath or clip him while he remains calm and gentle.

PITFALLS: Remember a horse cannot see under his nose, and his chest, the underside of his neck and top of his front legs can be blind spots (he can move his head to see if he wants to) so avoid introducing anything new to him there. The same applies to behind his tail, always make sure he knows you are there first before touching him.

CAN YOUR HORSE... stay still while you treat a minor cut on his hock when you are on your own and he is in the field among his mates?

LONG-TERM BENEFITS: In competition, your horse will be confident to stand still while there is lots of action going on close to him.

◁ Work like this ensures that Passion is happy to have her tail touched and to feel a rope around her rump, and that she accepts seeing Joanna in her other eye as she goes behind her

Exercise 5: Accepting your stick and other tools

Why? Through training your horse to be trusting and gentle with all your tools you will ensure that he never feels threatened when you use them. It is never safe to get on a horse unless he is gentle with you and your equipment. If he is afraid of your tools, he will not give an educated response to their use. This training, if done well, will also help a nervous or whip-shy horse. You can also use it to develop your horse's ability to cope with sudden or fast movement, such as running dogs, speeding cyclists, fast traffic, low-flying jets and helicopters.

⇧ Rachel teaches Charlie that a rope is safe, even around his legs and tail

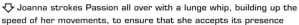

⇩ Joanna strokes Passion all over with a lunge whip, building up the speed of her movements, to ensure that she accepts its presence

How? IN HAND: Adopt and maintain soft, non-driving neutral body language. Then, following the principles given in exercise 4, begin to introduce the item you want him to gain confidence with – a stick, lunge whip, rope or saddle cloth. Work with him so that he accepts it touching him gently all over his body, including around his legs and under his feet where practical. Continue until you can drop it beside him and swing it around all over him with no change in his gentleness. Over several sessions, advance the difficulty until you are able, for example, to use a flag or a plastic bag on a stick at higher and higher speeds swinging and waving it all around and right beside him.

RIDDEN: Only once you have done the training in hand is it safe to progress to trying it ridden. Apply the same techniques moving your stick around and putting coats on and off, dropping clothing from him, picking it up from the ground with your stick, and so on.

HOW SHOULD IT FEEL? As though anything you are holding is non-threatening to the horse because it is an extension of you and, if your training has progressed well, you are his trusted leader and senior partner.

⬇ Flo is calm even though Daisy flaps a coat around her shoulders. This was achieved gradually, beginning with a small coat and work in hand

⬆ The Colt has learnt that fly spray is not threatening through advance and retreat training that began further away from him and on his body, eventually progressing to his neck and head

GOAL: To be able to use any of your tools at any speed to communicate with your horse confidently and to have him stay gentle with fast or sudden movement around him.

PITFALLS: No matter how good your horse has got at this exercise, never introduce new equipment in a hurry or on a stressful day. Allow the horse the dignity of a polite introduction to new things, especially if it smells of a strange horse.

CAN YOUR HORSE… let you crack a stock whip from his back?

LONG–TERM BENEFITS: Your horse won't baulk when you collect a rosette at a show, or when you're revising a dressage test while on his back or when high winds blow leaves across your path.

Neville the Rebel accepts Sweepy sitting on his bare back. This training would have begun with a rug between horse and dog. Horses are slippery and dogs have sharp claws, but with adequate gentling, this can be fun. You can teach your horse to accept almost anything – even whip cracking – with well planned training which progressively educates him.

Exercise 6: Responding to the go forward buttons

This exercise is divided into three individual lessons – separately introducing the three buttons that ask a horse to move forward: yielding forward from direct pull on the head; giving forward energy in response to an asking aid on the go button just behind the girth; moving away from 'pressure' on the go button behind the tail.

⬇ Rachel wriggles her stick to get Charlie's attention before stepping back (note her neutral body language)

⬇ As she backs away, she invites Charlie to come with her using drawing body language. He is a little late on the uptake, so the rope tightens, but he comes gently and well

⬇ Charlie is slow to stop, so Rachel blocks him to avoid him invading her space. Charlie stops before he gets too close

• Yielding forward from a direct pull on the halter

Why? This teaches your horse to respond correctly to pressure on the go button on his head and therefore to lead in hand or off another horse; it is also excellent training for tying up and loading.

How? IN HAND: Begin with the horse standing a few feet away from you. Stand and face him with neutral body language and a loose rope (about 2m/6ft of slack). Begin to back away from him encouraging him to follow using soft, drawing body language but holding the rope firmly. If he does not follow you he will soon meet the pressure from the tightening rope on the go button on the back of his head. Just hold on tight and wait for him to move towards you. Do not jerk at him. If his feet have got planted help him a bit by moving off to one side a little to unbalance him and free up his feet, but keep the pressure steady, strong and even – no more no less, even if he braces back into it – until the moment he moves just a foot forward, then instantly release all pressure from his head, relax and reward him. Repeat this, gradually building up the speed of your backward steps and increasing your expectation of the speed of his following you. Once he gets moving, you may need to be ready to block him to stop him walking into you at first! This exercise requires surprisingly good co-ordination and balance from you and the horse. Make sure you are far enough away for the horse to see your body language.

HOW SHOULD IT FEEL? As though the horse comes with you as soon as you put pressure on that go button, stops politely when you stop, and waits confidently near you.

GOAL: Eventually you should be able to work through the transitions fluidly from halt to rein back to forward to halt and so on with no pauses or jerks, in any situation, especially loading into a trailer.

PITFALLS: Beware of the dangers of pulling him into your space: a confused or anxious horse may barge at you with his shoulder so be ready to block him and send his shoulder away from you if necessary. If you inadvertently teach him to produce extra forward

Konker has not followed Joanna so meets pressure. She stays rounded and inviting, taking care not to glare into his eyes, waiting for him to move his feet towards her

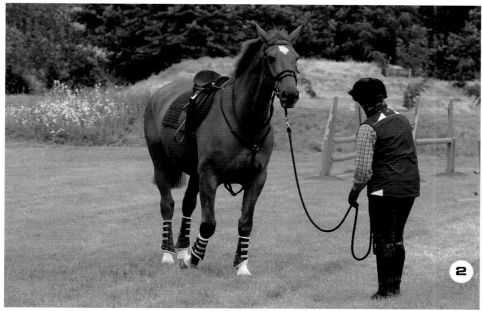

When Konker moves, it is a little to the side. However, Joanna decides to accept this try, and reward him with a release of pressure from the rope and her body language

energy before you have taught him to control his balance and stop or slow his feet down on request, you could be creating a problem for yourself in that he may walk all over you. If you have any problems, work back through your buttons and through exercises 1, 2 and 3, thoroughly, before attempting this again. Your job is to ensure you stay safe and to keep your horse out of your space – he should always stop politely before he gets too close to you.

CAN YOUR HORSE... move backwards and forwards and from one side over to the other, gently and easily at the touch of a button, even when tied up?

LONG-TERM BENEFITS: This is useful for everyday training but also for tying up, especially by the lorry when there are lots of other horses coming and going. Maybe even for leading your second-placed horse from your winner at the prize-giving ceremony!

- **Giving forward energy in response to an asking aid on the go button just behind the girth**

Why? This is the site of the main ridden go button (see p.43) – your most important button – and, if carefully trained and maintained, the horse will remain sensitive to it forever and he will be 'on the aids' or 'in front of the leg' whenever you like. He will be ready to start learning this when you have gained respect for the stop buttons, exercise 2, and make sure he is gentle to your tools, too, exercise 5.

How? IN HAND: First find his go button. Use your fingers to find the sensitive spot that he offers to move forward from. It is normally found low on his flank just behind where the girth would sit and where you will eventually use your leg to ask for go. You will need to experiment a little as each horse's natural go button is in a slightly different spot. Use energizing body language, align your body and point your centre towards this spot. With one hand, open up a space for him to move forward into and invite and ask him to move forward, in a curve or circle around you to begin with. If necessary, use stronger body language and the stick to put pressure on the site of the go button by pointing, nudging, tapping (go through the levels of pressure, see p.51) until you get the desired response and he moves forward. Instantly stop requesting and thank him; let him 'slide' and keep going for a few strides if he offers to do so, so that he knows

⇧ Pressure aimed towards the go button behind the girth means move your feet forward – go

he gave the correct response, then politely stop him and repeat, repeat, repeat. He may have stuttered to a stop anyway, and that's ok while he is learning; eventually he will understand to keep going. You may need to walk sideways to ensure your body alignment sends energy to his go button and matches your aids. Once he has got the idea of moving forward when asked, you can begin to ask him to walk in straight lines and turn to face forwards yourself.

RIDDEN: The techniques are very similar but ensure your body statement is a driving one and your body language says go: this means that your hands and arms are soft to allow the forward movement, that your body is tall, balanced and open-chested, and that your mental focus is forward. It is often a good idea to have a hand on the neckstrap in case his starts are jerky while he is learning. Ask him to move off; if you do have to use your legs, ensure your heels are well down to keep your leg muscles firm and use

⇩ Konker is reluctant to lead up beside Joanna so she turns to become more effective and taps him on his go button with the stick handle, inviting him forward. As he yields forwards and walks on Joanna moves sideways with him

⬆ Whiskers braces against Roger instead of moving forward as he asks

⬆ Roger moves out to the side to drive her forward off the go button, using a swing of the tail of the rope

both legs simultaneously and equally for straightness, progressing from a touch to a nudge to a kick. If he ignores this then use the stick lightly as well as the leg. Again, as with the in-hand work, persist nudging or kicking with the legs or tapping or smacking with the stick until you get the desired result, then instantly stop asking, thank him and continue as above. Always use a light aid first, no matter how often you have to repeat the ask to keep him sensitive, but use the stick if he does not respond to a light kick – thumping at his ribs with your legs is poor training and undignified.

HOW SHOULD IT FEEL? A good response should feel like a soft, controlled surge of forward energy on request in response to a touch on his go button.

GOAL: When working in hand – to have your horse going off a light touch confidently and easily on either rein, until you can just point the end of the rope or tail of the lunge whip towards that spot to get forward movement or more impulsion.

When riding – to have him responding and staying lightly in front of the leg and answering the go button with confidence and enthusiasm.

PITFALLS: Try not to fall into the temptation of putting pressure too far back along his flanks or on his hindquarters to get forward movement because that is not the go button but the hindquarters-move-over button and he will quite rightly swing his quarters away in response. Also, avoid confusing him about the go button and flex button by cultivating a slightly different spot, feel and intention for each button (see p.42). Be aware that this is the beginning of asking the horse

to give you some of his precious life-saving energy and impulsion on request (see p.22). Accept this with gratitude and use it with care, so that you gain his respect and trust. Ask him to stay gentle in the rein as you move off. Use lateral flexion if necessary during the transition (see exercise 10 for more information).

CAN YOUR HORSE… move up into canter from halt without any bracing from you or him?

LONG–TERM BENEFITS: You can have your horse staying softly in front of the leg for the whole dressage test or easily press him forward to take a stride out in the jump off.

⬇ Julie's leg is in exactly the right place to ask Konker to go forward. Her focus is good and her body and hands are allowing the go

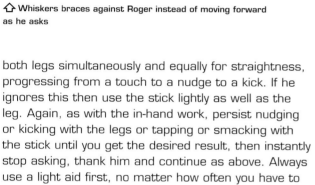

• Moving away from 'pressure' on the go button behind the tail

Why? This educates your horse to move away from pressure behind him, rather than to follow his instinct and kick out. If he thought he was being threatened in the wild – say a lion was clinging onto his bottom – his life would depend on his pushing back and kicking fast with both hindlegs. Teaching him to move softly forward from pressure behind him is another step in gentling your horse.

How? IN HAND: Adopt driving body language that says go and align your body so you point your centre behind his tail. Stand facing him but out to one side, then with your hand invite him to move forward as you open up a space for him to move forward into. Swing the end of the whip or rope to create activity behind his tail until he moves forward, then stop asking him, but allow him to slide forward a little, to confirm he has done the right thing, before asking him to stop. Give him a little soak time as a reward and then repeat the lesson. When doing this exercise beware that horses, even those you know and trust, can kick so make sure you are outside the kick zone.

HOW SHOULD IT FEEL? Like an increase in energy, offered smoothly and willingly, from an aid given behind his tail.

GOAL: To have a horse that moves forward confidently from pressure behind his tail, which is very useful when lunging or loose schooling. To have a horse that is relaxed about activity behind him.

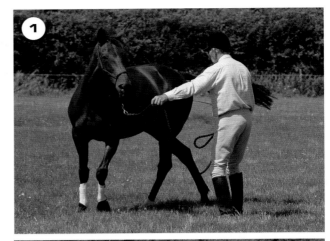

⇧ 1) Roger asks Whisky to move out onto a circle by pointing his centre behind her tail while allowing her to move forward with his left hand
2) He continues inviting her forward with a soft hand and increases the pressure behind her by swinging the rope
3) Roger repeats the swing again – he moves his centre to face her ribs, which she yields in flexion, and she moves forward from his ask

⇦ Joanna is working with The Colt, sending him forward with a lunge whip behind his tail. Her centre points at his ribs to ask for lateral flexion, which she gets – an example of soft, forward lunging with no gadgets, although The Colt could track up behind a little more

⬆ Other things can become go signals behind the tail, too, either intentionally or accidentally

PITFALLS: The horse must move calmly straight forward away from the pressure behind him and not crash around in circles trying to escape the threat. If he tries to push into you, block his head with one arm while sending his tail away with the other.

CAN YOUR HORSE… stay gentle and get on with his work while keeping out of the way of an upset horse behind him in the crowded collecting ring?

LONG–TERM BENEFITS: In a crowd or a crisis this skill helps to prevent your horse kicking or squashing people because he will know that he can move forward to get away from the pressure at any time if he feels he needs to.

⬅ A rude or anxious horse can have a kick zone 4m (12ft) behind his body. Always work outside this area

Exercise 7: Cultivating the hindquarters-move-over button – turn on the forehand

Why? The horse's engine is in his hindquarters, therefore control of them is crucial for having overall control of his physical movement and energy. This exercise teaches him the 'hindquarters-move-over' button (p.43) by asking him to step his hindquarters away around his stationary shoulders. A horse's feet are his getaway equipment and by relinquishing control of them to you he shows he is trusting your leadership (see p.18). By having a horse politely move his hind feet you will earn respect, and by appreciating his efforts you will gain even more of his trust. Moving the hindquarters on their own is best not done before the previous exercises as you may end up with an unbalanced or stressed horse toppling into your lap because he may not have sufficient emotional or physical self-control to be able to back off.

How? IN HAND: With one hand on his lead rope or rein to block forward movement, adopt driving body language by aligning and pointing your centre towards his hip. Walk towards his hip as though you were going to walk right through it, asking him to move it away from you. Put pressure on his hindquarters-move-over button or swing a rope or stick at it if necessary, while still using body language pressure to move his hip. Instantly release the pressure and stop asking the second he moves his quarters away. When you repeat the exercise, progressively move the hindquarters-move-over button closer to the place where your leg will ask for the movement – a few inches behind the girth. Once this is established on both sides you can begin to ask for this ridden, too.

⬆ To prevent further forward movement she uses blocking body language and moves her quarters-over pressure to behind the girth. She accepts his try with a brief yes.

⬆ After a couple more steps, The Colt is more balanced and not pushing through Joanna's hand so much. She is now only using her centre and intention to move his quarters over – a good reduction in the level of pressure required

⬆ Finishing the turn, The Colt halts squarely over all four feet. Joanna steps back to acknowledge his try and allow his bow, lick and chew. Her centre and arm are soft. Yes, thank you!

⬆ Joanna asks The Colt to move his quarters over by using pressure at his hip. He crosses his hind legs well but has pushed forward through her hand a little

RIDDEN: It is preferable to cultivate the hindquarters-move-over button in hand before attempting it ridden. Think through what you want him to do before you begin. Hold his forehand still, perhaps placing him facing a fence to block him and to help him keep his balance, and ask him to move his quarters around, one step at a time. Use pressure and release aids with your leg on the hindquarters-move-over button and maybe a flappy stick to tap him around (again, this is 'Riding the Wave', see p.45). Keep your own balance and take your time.

1) Starting the turn from a good balanced halt, Caroline asks Jill to move with her left leg while her right leg is ready to help keep the shoulders still and her right hand blocks forward movement
2) Jill moves around well crossing her hind feet over each other
3) Here there is a pause as the mare is a little stuck. Caroline's left hip has dropped as she uses too strong a leg aid – a light tap with a stick would be more effective
4) Although they are moving again, Caroline's leg is still a little strong. Ideally the horse should move off a light aid

HOW SHOULD IT FEEL? Not chaotic! A well prepared turn feels easy and balanced performed fluently, a step at a time.

GOAL: To have a horse that understands the use of the hindquarters-move-over button progressing eventually through from the novice to the advanced spot (see p.43). To be able to do a perfect turn on the forehand, with the inner hindleg crossing fluently in front of the outer one, and the front legs not pivoting but marking time and stepping around in a tiny circle.

PITFALLS: Beware of confusing the horse by being unclear with your aids or buttons or rushing him. Go one step at a time.

CAN YOUR HORSE… execute an easy turn on the forehand while you open and close a gate?

LONG-TERM BENEFITS: Cultivating this button gives you improved control of the quarters and hind feet.

Exercise 8: Leading and exercising in hand

Why? This exercise teaches your horse to walk beside you, politely, stopping and starting when you do. I like my horse where I can see him, where I can easily yield his shoulder away from me and keep his hooves away from my toes. If he is behind you and you trip or he jumps forward, you have a wreck. You are training your horse to respect you as his leader, but that does not mean he has to follow behind you physically. Although there is an emotional link to the person who is physically leading the way, he can still learn

to respect you even if he is ahead. Practice makes perfect with this exercise; it is a great test of your co-ordination.

How? IN HAND: Begin beside a fence and standing facing your horse. Adopting energizing and drawing body language and using the stop and go buttons and those for moving the hindquarters and forequarters over, invite your horse to walk along beside you by walking backwards and sideways leading him in your left hand. If he is reluctant to come up beside you on what is now your left side, put pulling pressure on his head and use your right hand to swing the rope tail

⬆ Joanna is taking Konker out to the training field and she is prepared to block him if he pushes through the gateway

⬆ He is a bit keen, so she blocks him and jerks backwards on the rope to slow him. She doesn't hold him too tight; she is just asking him to slow and be polite, using his own self-control

⬆ This works and he becomes calmer and more gentle – good boy

⬆ Joanna turns and they walk on normally and politely

or stick towards the go button on his right side or behind his tail. The moment he walks up beside you, release the pressure on his head and go buttons and carry on walking backwards. Repeat the pressures as necessary, preferring the go button to the pull on the halter/reins but combining them as you think best. To stop him use strong upright blocking body language and point your centre in front of him to warn him you mean him to stop and then halt square. If he ignores you and goes on past, tug sharply at his head jerking the rope backwards until he stops. If he still ignores you, swing your rope tail and/or stick in front of him to block him until he stops – you may need to walk swiftly backwards and sideways to keep beside

him. Once he has got the idea, turn around and walk forwards with him beside you in your right hand as normal, swapping over hands and reverting to this Effective Training method if any crisis seems likely to occur. Remember to train him to lead in either hand; this is especially important if you plan to lead on the road, where you need him in your kerbside hand for safety.

⬆ In his anxiety he nearly bursts through her hand, so she turns and swaps hands to be more effective. She uses her left hand to block his push, and right hand to block his shoulder from knocking her down

⬆ Roger leading The Colt. The pair are working in partnership – the result of much schooling

HALTER BREAKING AND LEADING FOALS

*To start halter breaking any horse you need to begin with teaching him to yield to pressure (see exercise 2), then progress through the exercises before you teach him to lead forward. In early leading lessons, a schoolmaster horse is useful to demonstrate how it should be done and give an inexperienced horse confidence.

*Never pull forward on a young foal's head as his instinct is to brace and flip over backwards. Teach a foal to yield first using a soft towel around his neck and asking him to move towards his mother. Yield slightly to one side, not straight ahead. When you think he is ready to use a halter, remember how sensitive the whiskers are and acclimatize him to the feel of the halter first with a soft hand. Keep sessions short – five minutes maximum. Some foals are ready to begin learning at birth, others not until they are three weeks old – the earlier you begin, the more fun your foal will be.

⬆ Beginning by just asking Primmore's Patience to yield his head

HOW SHOULD IT FEEL? As though the horse reads your thoughts and stays with you politely, not pushing or pulling, just light and easy.

GOAL: A horse that willingly and politely walks or trots beside you in any situation, on either side, in hand or from another horse.

PITFALLS: Avoid confusing the horse by dragging him and not letting him find a release from the pressure. It takes a lot of schooling for a horse to become good at leading. Also beware that your stopping aids do not unintentionally become driving aids.

CAN YOUR HORSE… be polite when asked to trot up for the vet on a wet and windy day?

LONG-TERM BENEFITS: This prepares your horse to be led effortlessly round the main ring at a prize-giving ceremony.

1) Rachel asks Charlie to yield around in a curve and a turn by pushing his hindquarters away and drawing his head towards her; 2) Then she asks him to follow her using pressure and release but keeps going to show him that he can lead without having to be pulled; 3) Rachel reminds Charlie to keep up; 4) Success! Charlie is happy to lead anywhere on a light contact; 5) They put their new skills to good use

↥ Pudding trots up well with June on her offside, ready for leading up the road or off another horse

By asking your horse to always keep his head towards you and with the use of good drawing body language you will find you will be able to lead your horse without a line. Mark Rodney the Australian horseman calls this 'leading by a whisker'. Once your groundwork on a line is really good and your horse seeks to stay with you, you can unclip the rope and just draw him to you with your body language, executing small turns and curves, never turning your back to him, and progress from there until you can lead him anywhere 'by a whisker'. Use just your drawing hand to lead him with nothing but an imaginary silk thread – true partnership.

Exercise 9: Teaching a square halt and gaining control of all four feet

⬇ Julie asks Konker to move backwards over a pole on the ground. By doing so he gives her control of his feet. Note her body language, which is accepting his try while continuing to work. Soak time is next

Why? This simple exercise reinforces the understanding and use of all the buttons learned so far and develops trust and confidence as well as the horse's ability to halt anywhere required. The practical reason for this exercise is to gain the ability to put your horse's feet anywhere you ask, including halting square; the emotional benefit is that by relinquishing his ability to flee, and therefore entrusting you with his life, he is further accepting your good leadership.

How? IN HAND: You will need a solid board, heavy tarpaulin or old carpet. Adopt appropriate body language and, using all the different buttons as required, simply ask your horse to place just one front foot onto your chosen item, using increasing levels of pressure as necessary (p.51). This is a big ask, because horses do not readily put their feet onto 'unsafe' ground. When he does as he is asked, it is important to instantly release all the pressure and accept the halt, even though only one foot is on the 'mat'. Timing is vital, which is why this is such good training for us humans too! This exercise is not as easy as it sounds and he will find a thousand ways to evade you, but use the buttons and your tools and skills clearly, persistently, patiently and fairly and you will succeed. Once you have one front foot on back him off again and have some soak time before progressing to asking for two then three feet and

eventually, and significantly, all four. He will try hard to have you accept just three feet because by giving you all four, he is completely trusting you with his life. This work can be broken up into several little lessons. Once he can halt square on your chosen surface, you will find it easy to achieve a good halt anywhere. This is great training for competition horses.

RIDDEN: Apply a blocking forward movement body statement to ask the horse to stop: close your thighs to the saddle, sit still, keeping a good tall and light posture. Be especially careful not to lose balance and fall behind the vertical, making a forward driving aid. If your horse ignores your body statement, apply constant and consistent pressure to his mouth stop button and wait for him to stop. Match like with like in

⬇ Passion is about to give Joanna her final foot, having placed the other three on the board. Joanna is accepting her try

⬆ Square halts are a useful skill for ponies – Pudding practises

GOAL: Through good timing and good use of your buttons and pressure and release techniques you should soon have your horse offering to do anything you ask. This exercise will also help you to have a horse that will happily stand on a bridge while the traffic or water hurtles below him.

PITFALLS: When doing this exercise in the saddle, beware of raising his head to stop him – it is his feet you need to control. When riding, the only place you can apply pressure in front of his feet is to the stop button in his mouth, which means that if the head comes up, the feet and shoulders may try to keep going. Remember the response to the stop button should be to stop the feet and an anxious horse will always want one foot ahead of the other ready to flee. He needs to learn to trust you enough to 'park up' for you.

CAN YOUR HORSE… place his feet just where the physiotherapist might want them?

LONG–TERM BENEFITS: With a horse that has learnt this exercise you can maintain a perfect halt at X at the end of a dressage test with the crowd clapping and cheering, or ask him to stand perfectly during the winner's ceremony.

the resistance; when he does stop, instantly release the pressure. If he topples over repeat the pressure and release when he stops. Allow him to stand unaided in self-carriage over all four feet for a few moments of soak time, then repeat. Walk, halt, thank you – soak. You are teaching him that when you ask him, he should stop his feet, remaining in front of the leg and softly awaiting the signal to move off.

HOW SHOULD IT FEEL? As though the horse is really well balanced over all four feet and able and ready to stop and stand in a square halt on request, anywhere. When ridden, this exercise is the equivalent of a dressage halt, the horse carrying the rider in a good outline with a strong back and squared feet – you should feel he has plenty of impulsion at the ready.

⇨ After testing Roger's leadership by trying to evade him, Whisky steps onto the board. Roger asks Whisky for a square halt and to stand awaiting the next move. The board enables the rider to hear when all four feet have halted

1

2

Exercise 10: Achieving bend and suppleness – the lateral flexion buttons

Why? The aim is to develop a polite and supple horse that can move forward with elasticity and engagement. The exercise asks your horse to flex his ribs away, so that his body has a banana-like bend. Although this is often called yielding the ribs because this is what it feels like, a horse cannot really bend his ribs, only contract or extend his muscles (see 'Footfall – Engaging and Lateral Work', p.88).

How? IN HAND: Ask your horse to halt square beside you, then find the lateral flex button, usually located just behind the girth, a little behind and above the go button (see p.43). Aligning your body to point your centre at

his ribs, go through the pressure levels (see p.51) with your fingers or stick touching the button until you get the right response – a bend of the ribs and neck while he stands still – then instantly release the pressure, accept the try and reward your horse with a little soak time. Repeat, repeat, repeat, seeking to use lighter aids each time. Develop his response in the halt at this stage but once you have taught him how to circle politely (Exercise 13) you can use this button to gain an inside bend when lunging and whenever you feel him stiffening, spooking or bracing his ribs against you, progressing to leg yield and shoulder in.

RIDDEN: As for in hand, but from the saddle. Begin in halt. Use your leg on the lateral flexion button and hand on the rein and he should yield his head around towards your knee – if he does, rub his face for him in appreciation. Be accurate and consistent with your aids, which is more difficult from the saddle. If the horse's response is slow, use a tickle of the stick on the lateral flex button, supported by some light

⇩ Syd and JP using lateral work to develop hindleg engagement in the Burghley collecting ring, early in the morning, before the crowds appear

↥ Preparing in hand before asking for leg yield when ridden

CAN YOUR HORSE… allow you to control even where he looks, by flexing from your hand or leg aid on the lateral flex button, bending softly from his tail to his nose?

LONG-TERM BENEFITS: The suppleness you create in the neck, ribs and pelvis will allow not only superb lateral work but also engagement of sufficient impulsion from each hindleg in turn to produce a high-scoring extended trot in dressage. In jumping, you'll be able to change your horse's bend at the touch of a button for extra tight turns.

pressure on the mouth to teach him what you want – don't thump with the leg. Cease asking the moment he gives the desired response, straighten him up and have quiet still moment of soak time before you ask for another flex.

HOW SHOULD IT FEEL? When you press the lateral flexion button the horse should yield his ribs away and bring his head around, like a good soft banana.

GOAL: A supple horse that easily allows you to control his bend – leading to good easy lateral work.

PITFALLS: Beware of the horse moving away rather than bending, or getting this button confused with the go button or move over buttons. Clarity is essential. If he is finding it hard to bend, begin with just moving his head, then progress to a shoulder yield to move the shoulder out of the way then ask for rib flexion again. If you get in a muddle, revise all the earlier exercises and buttons before you try again. Be sure the neck bend is easy in hand and ridden before you ask for the ribs to flex.

↥ Pippa Funnell has control of all four of Primmore's Pride's feet and his flexion – a perfect example

Exercise 11: Moving sideways on a circle – leg yield

Why? This exercise works with an exaggeration of the lateral flexion button, in the same way that rein back is an exaggeration of the halt button (Exercise 2). It involves a lot of self-carriage and moving your horse's feet, but once mastered is quite easy for you to ask for, anywhere. It introduces the horse to his move-over-sideways buttons, by putting pressure on his flank and asking him to respond to the shoulders- and hindquarters-move-over buttons and the lateral flexion buttons, together with a little bit of go button, in quick succession without toppling over onto you. As it is very complicated for your horse, be sure to give very clear signals and be patient. The exercise continues to give your leadership validity as it is progressively working towards gaining easier control of his feet, essential for manoeuvrability and dressage. It is a good leadership renewal exercise so it is very useful after a scare or a muddle and is particularly helpful in defusing a crisis. A horse cannot rear or buck when his hind feet are not behind his shoulder.

Riding with your hands wide apart is an excellent way of coping in an emergency or helping a nervous horse to stay within your aids, but avoid using this strategy all the time. Your horse should be able to stay between hands held in the normal position – a straight line from your elbow through your forearm to the bit. If you work in emergency mode most of the time what will you use as extra when there is real crisis? This applies to all your training: allow the horse the choice of right or wrong and let him learn from his mistakes and successes

so that he stays on the aids of his own free will and not because you have forced him by allowing him no escape. This is usually more of a problem with very effective riders, so the better you are, the more you need to beware of this syndrome. Don't shout when you can whisper!

▽ Joanna is asking The Colt to yield sideways by putting pressure along his side. She stays in the middle, so he moves around her like the hands of a clock. Thank you!

How? IN HAND: You will be asking your horse to move around in a circle from halt, stepping sideways and facing you in the centre. Stand in front of him ready with blocking body language; place your hand on the back of his halter or bridle with your arm held very straight so that the elbow is locked to apply pressure to the stop button if required. Ask him to move his shoulder, then his ribs, then his quarters over in quick succession. Keep on asking on the three buttons until he gives you the right response and steps sideways, even with only one foot, instantly release the pressure and allow him to stay still and balanced over his feet while you both pause for a little soak time. Repeat – ask, move over, thanks – until he easily moves sideways around you standing still in the centre of the circle, one step at a time, slowly, softly and almost straight in his body like the hands of a clock, crossing his legs over neatly in pairs.

RIDDEN: This is an advanced ridden exercise because it involves so many buttons, but this is why it is excellent for calming worried horses because they have to think about their feet, and not about the 'tigers' all around them. To help him the first few times stand him with his head facing a wall or fence. Block

⬆ Konker is pushing forward so Joanna has blocked his forward movement and asks him to yield sideways, which he does quite politely

forward movement through your body statement – sit still keeping a good, tall and light posture, be especially careful not to lose balance and fall sideways or behind the vertical and so become a hindrance. To move him clockwise, ask him to flex in a banana shape to the right using your right leg on the lateral flexion button and then receive and hold this right bend in your right hand. Move the right leg to apply pressure, with your heel well down, behind the girth – or even

FOOTFALL – ENGAGING AND LATERAL WORK

*A horse can only respond correctly to the leg aid to move over sideways if it is applied just before he lifts that foot off the ground so the timing of your leg aids needs to be carefully used in rhythm with his feet.

*A horse's spine cannot bend laterally, but his ribs can contract and stretch, and his shoulders, neck and pelvis can flex, so he can make a banana shape.

*A horse uses his ribs to express himself and can push them at you, hold them rudely rigid or politely soft. Softening the ribs is a great offering and you should show much appreciation if he gives it.

further back along his flank if he is a novice, to ask him to move over to the right. Keep up the annoying pressure by rhythmically and consistently pressing, nudging, tapping, flapping, kicking or even smacking (gradually increase the levels of pressure as usual) and wait for him to move his ribs and quarters over to the right while maintaining a left bend. When he does move, instantly release the pressure, sit very still and soft and give him a rub. Ask him to stand unaided with slight left flexion in self-carriage over all four feet for a few moments of soak time, then repeat – ask, move, thanks. Now do the exercise on the other side. You need to have a dexterous inside leg because it has to maintain flexion at the girth, ask the horse to move using the quarters-move-over button behind the girth and control the shoulders using the shoulder-move-over button on the girth.

Once he can manage this from the halt then you can use a less angled version in the other paces – a full sideways leg yield on the circle.

Joanna begins by asking The Colt to look to the centre of the circle with his inside eye and to yield a few steps sideways with her inside leg

Once he has the idea she progresses to asking him to look to the inside with both eyes while yielding him sideways on a circle for a few steps. Smile Joanna!

HOW SHOULD IT FEEL? Calm, slow and a bit like a sideways slide. It is not that hard for the horse if his body is not too bent and he is gentle in mind and body.

GOAL: To have a horse that easily and happily steps sideways on request in leg yield or shoulder-in.

PITFALLS: Avoid confusing the horse or yourself by using complex aids. Ask politely and clearly using just what it takes to get the right result – worry about how pretty it looks when you get more used to the manoeuvre. This exercise has a powerful effect on the horse so we are always careful to whom we teach it, lest they should abuse it, and by putting it in here we are entrusting you with that care too.

CAN YOUR HORSE… move sideways into a narrow gateway, and so out of the way of a fast oncoming car?

LONG–TERM BENEFITS: In dressage you will have a wonderful shoulder-in or leg yield. This is a brilliant suppling exercise, especially for teaching a horse to swing his ribs over to the side so that his inside hindleg can come further under him to engage more easily for collection, extended trot and flying changes one day.

Training your horse to move sideways greatly improves your safety on the public highway by enabling you to escape potentially dangerous situations by yielding your horse sideways out of harm's way. Although young and inexperienced, Passion is a very safe conveyance, even on slippery roads, as she is easily controlled having been started and developed using Effective Training. Here she is calmly waiting as good as gold aged only four having just arrived at her second 'party'.

⬇ JP asks Syd to work with just a neck bend

⬇ Nick demonstrates the next stage – leg yield in trot in circles and straight lines

Exercise 12: Teaching teardrop turns and half circles

Why? This is a preparation exercise for lunging or riding and puts into practice all your control of the shoulders, quarters and sideways steps by using nearly all the buttons. It is also excellent for building up a horse's balance, athleticism and physical and emotional self-control and it is great fun to do! (Read about working in tight spaces, p.148, before you begin.)

1) Joanna asks The Colt to back away to about 2.7m (9ft) distance
2) She invites The Colt onto a left half circle and he responds with good soft ribs and feet
3) and 4) Joanna asks The Colt to move his ribs and quarters away

How? IN HAND: You will be using a quick succession of different aids so a stick is almost essential for accuracy in the early days. Things happen fast in this exercise. To execute a left 10m (30ft) half circle and turn, stand with your back to a wall or fence with the horse on your right, facing you, about 2.7m (9ft) away. Point your centre at his chest to block him from approaching you and then invite him to move out to a half circle to your left by sweeping your left arm out and around to the side (I call this a 'Sir Francis Drake' invitation because it's

5) and 6) She then draws his head to turn and face her
7) He is a little close... 8) ...so she asks him to move back
9) He responds well and they have a little soak time 10) Joanna now asks The Colt to begin the return half circle to the right (cont. overleaf)

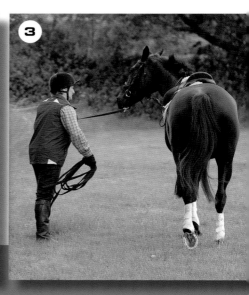

IRISH ROOTS

This exercise is reminiscent of the classic Irish technique where two people stand either side of a bank. One lunges the horse over the bank and the other turns him around and sends him back. This simple schooling technique has produced some of the most brilliant jumping horses in the world but seems to have been forgotten recently, especially since loose jumping in round pens became fashionable, which so often involves using a whip to scare the young horse over the fence and seems to produce very nervous horses.

how he might fling a cape out to cover a puddle for a queen to step on) at the same time sending him out with your driving body language and line or stick if necessary. Keep him in walk and as he nears the wall or fence on your left side, point your centre to his chest using sending body language to block him from moving towards you and point your stick or swing your line towards his hip to send his hindquarters away and then draw his head around to face you (you only need to soften your centre very slightly to do this). Use a strong blocking body statement to warn him you mean him to stop and then ask him to halt square facing you as close to the wall or fence as possible. You may need to yield him over sideways to achieve this. (Doing

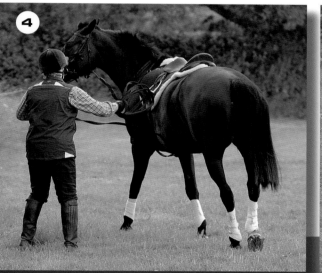

this exercise beside a fence or wall means he will have to stop at some point anyway.) You want him to stand as close to the wall as you think is fair – about 1–2m (3–6ft) away – facing you, balanced and ready for the next request. Hopefully, if you give him space and time, he will lower his head and bow to you and maybe lick and chew because by asking him to move sideways and stand so close to the wall you have asked him for a big try. Be sure to appreciate and reward his effort. Next invite him with your right hand to go out on a 10m (30ft) half circle to the right; as he gets to the wall, repeat the manoeuvres that you did on the other rein. Keep everything slow and dignified because you

are asking for a lot of co-ordination from both you and the horse. Keep practising until this becomes easy, rewarding with plenty of soak time.

RIDDEN: Proceed as for in hand but using the riding buttons. This is quite advanced for the rider as it involves so many different aids, but it is also fun to do and young horses seem to find it quite easy, providing they have time to think and the block of the wall to turn them. You can progress up to making this even more advanced by doing the turns away from the wall or fence, eventually at higher speeds and with jumps too.

11) and 12) Joanna asks The Colt to stay out on the circle and blocks his attempts to hurry

13) and 14) The Colt begins to lose his good banana shape, but recovers and finishes well. Joanna accepts his try

HOW SHOULD IT FEEL? A bit rough and ready at first until co-ordination and use of buttons is perfected but eventually wonderful, like ballroom dancing with your horse as he balances and engages behind, turning and moving in half circles at your request. Horses enjoy this exercise as it shows off all their skills.

GOAL: To be able to perform half circles and teardrop turns elegantly at the canter in a wide open space.

PITFALLS: The horse may get confused if you hurry or are unclear which button to press when, or if you are unco-ordinated. Revise all the previous exercises and then try again.

⬇ 'Did I do ok?' Yes, thank you, is followed by a good rub

CAN YOUR HORSE... do a half circle over a pole, do a teardrop turn easily, and canter back in a half circle over the same pole?

LONG-TERM BENEFITS: Most buttons and skills you need for your basic schooling are used in this one manoeuvre. For jumping practice this exercise simplifies work over poles or jumps in a confined space and avoids the horse having to make endless circles.

Exercise 13: Lunging in self-carriage and schooling in soft circles

Why? This exercise asks your horse to allow you to control his feet at any speed, in any direction, and at any time, using all the different buttons. When done well, it is a great way of earning his respect, but you must remember who is training whom and who is moving whom. Lunging well is also a wonderful way of developing the horse's self-carriage.

When you lunge or circle, you are looking for the horse to offer a soft rounded outline and self-carriage, while he is balanced over all four feet, working in an even rhythm and has soft inside flexion in the ribs and neck. As your horse becomes more advanced, you can improve his ability to work in an outline, with more impulsion and engaging his hindquarters, from collection to extension still working softly in just a halter or bridle. And all this can be done through skilled use of your buttons and body language.

A NEW EXPERIENCE

For many people, to have a horse circle around them offering soft banana-shaped lateral flexion in a good outline, with well balanced, soft, regular steps in just a halter is a real treat, especially if they have done years of traditional lunging and long reining. The closer your partnership with your horse becomes, the more the old methods seem to become less and less appropriate, with their reliance on a variety of clumsy gadgets that lack feel and finesse.

⬇ Passion yields well to my request – made with the rope end – for more lateral flexion. However, she looks a little worried so I keep my body language very soft

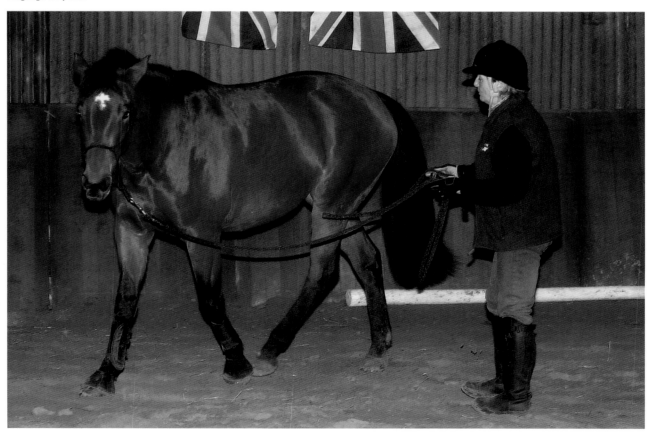

How? IN HAND: Begin by standing in the middle of the intended circle (keep it small and within reach of your stick at first, less than 10m/30ft). Ask the horse to walk slowly around you with an inviting 'Sir Francis Drake' sweep of the arm (see p.91) showing the direction you want him to go in. If he gets too close to you, use sending body language and point your centre at the offending button. If he tries to crowd you use your stick to block and send his head away, then his neck, shoulder and ribs, while putting pressure on the go button on his flank to get enough forward movement. If he tries to charge off, halt him as you did in exercise 12 or by bumping the rope, putting the stick in front of him and using blocking body language. He will turn to face you, which is fine at this stage, so long as he stops. You may need to frequently remind him to maintain his

Once your horse is working kindly on larger circles, and transitions to and from canter are easy, try including a pole on the ground. It is then wiser to progress by walking over a raised pole and using tear drop turns before trotting and eventually going into canter work on the circle. This training can take a few sessions; keep these sessions short and sweet, and ensure there is nothing on which the rope can snag beside the jump. Here the very experienced Skiver shows just how it is done!

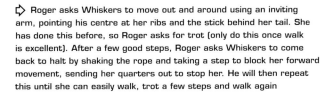

▷ Roger asks Whiskers to move out and around using an inviting arm, pointing his centre at her ribs and the stick behind her tail. She has done this before, so Roger asks for trot (only do this once walk is excellent). After a few good steps, Roger asks Whiskers to come back to halt by shaking the rope and taking a step to block her forward movement, sending her quarters out to stop her. He will then repeat this until she can easily walk, trot a few steps and walk again

Developing your own fearless horse

balance, speed and inside flexion by using the buttons. Once he can walk politely around you in a small circle with a good continuous inside flexion from nose to tail, try stopping properly. Do this in the same way as with the leading (exercise 8). Use a strong upright body statement to warn him you mean to ask him to stop and then step sideways and forwards to keep ahead of him and block him. If he ignores you and goes on past you at all, tug or bump sharply at his head until he stops. If he still ignores you, swing your rope and or stick from your right hand in front of him to block him until he stops. Make sure your body language is not sending him on and that you stay slightly ahead of him – move sideways quickly to keep ahead of him and avoid inadvertently driving him on. Although it is best to try not to let his quarters swing away so he halts on the perimeter of the circle; this is quite advanced, so a final sharp request for him to stop could be to send his quarters out and draw his head to you: he will screech to a halt facing you because sending the quarters out removes his engine. Accept this for the first few attempts then progress up to asking for the halt on a circle using a perimeter fence and good body language to help him halt square and not turn his hindquarters out and his shoulders in.

Consistency, persistence and dexterity are required here, but it is worth it – this form of lunging or working on a line may be a lot more difficult for you to learn but is infinitely better training for you and your horse, especially if you are preparing for dressage work. Trot only when halt and walk are easy on both reins. Again, start with a small circle and gradually enlarge it. Initially, do a just few steps of trot before asking for walk again. Likewise, progress to canter when trot is easy. Gradually increase the difficulty of your demands and the intensity of the impulsion and energy required, and include jumps, too. Like all lunging, this is a great way to prepare a young horse for riding or just to school or exercise him.

RIDDEN: These same circles are an excellent ridden schooling exercise and especially useful at the start of work, or when working in, to ensure a soft and forward horse.

⬇ Use the stick to push out any part of the horse that is coming in too close to you. Use it in front of the horse to slow or stop him, too

◁ Roger runs straight beside Charlie while he jumps. Roger will then stop and Charlie will circle around him. This is a preferable way to lunge jump when the horse is prone to hurrying

PITFALLS: Be sure to stand still and have him move around you. It only takes a few moments for the horse to start lunging you if your body language is weak or disorganized and you allow him to move you around! (If your horse ignores you or goes into rude lunge mode revise all the previous exercises, or see p.126.)

CAN YOUR HORSE... lunge politely and softly on a windy hilltop close to the start of the cross-country course?

LONG-TERM BENEFITS: This is a brilliant way to prepare your horse physically and mentally, even at a competition, especially if you have limited riding time.

HOW SHOULD IT FEEL? Like synchronized circling as the horse reads your body language and offers soft forward work for you – enjoy the partnership.

GOAL: To have a horse that can lunge around you in just a halter or bridle in both directions on any size circle, large or small, in any pace, with varied amounts of impulsion or speed and remain balanced supple and flexed at all times. That is true respect and partnership between human and horse – wow!

▽ The Colt offers soft forward work. As she reaches to reward him, Joanna's contact is a bit light and she is in danger of being tripped up

Exercise 14: Maintaining contact and following the feel

Why? As you progress to more educated aids and your horse becomes more responsive, you can begin to ask him to follow the feel when responding to your aids, such as following the inside leg aid through a turn, or working softly into a rein contact in medium trot. Horses will seek the place of least resistance but for maximum performance they need to be trained to stay softly on the aids and follow the feel, not to drop behind it. Following the feel is a delicate balance between releasing the pressure and avoiding the contact; this requires a good sense of feel and timing, along with all your horsemanship skills. During this work, it is important that the trainer or rider, as the leader, starts and ends every movement properly and does not allow the horse to drift into or out of any of them. It is also good to work in accurate patterns as this establishes the leadership – like ballroom dancers again!

How? IN HAND AND RIDDEN:
Decide what movements you will be doing; circles, transitions, leg yield or shoulder in on the circle are good ones for this exercise. Apply pressure on the appropriate buttons, one at a time in quick succession. Once the horse responds correctly then keep your aids softly in contact as you continue in the same way. By this stage your horse should be polite and confident enough not to try to fall behind the contact or run away from an aid. Ask him to continue in the movement for a few steps, but instead of releasing all pressure when he obliges, as you did in

CONTACT

Acceptance of feel and contact is one of the major differences between what is called 'English'-style performance work, and 'Western'-style practical horsemanship and stock work. It is not necessary to learn both styles; choose whichever suits your needs. Mostly due to the difference in the saddles and bridles, English riding requires higher levels of balance and training in the rider, for him or her to be safe enough to enjoy riding. In English-style riding, impulsion and engagement are very important, requiring feel and contact to contain and control this store of energy. They are vital in eventing, dressage, show jumping or cross country. This type of training is described as 'English' and is used all around the world.

In Western horsemanship the horse stays behind the bit with no contact, in self-carriage on a light rein. For transporting people or stock work the horse needs to be able to stop, go and turn in the most economical way and Western-style horsemanship has developed all around the world to fulfill those needs, but it is not suitable for jumping or dressage, because of the importance of contact and feel in these disciplines.

⇩ Joanna is asking The Colt to follow the feel of her aids as she asks him to move sideways and forwards. He is responding well

⇩ Syd is learning to follow JP's hand and leg asking him to bend but keep his feet still

his early training, keep a soft feel in the hand and the leg, thinking yes and maintaining the movement. After a few more steps take him out of the movement, rest a little and then repeat. You need to keep a contact, otherwise the horse cannot 'feel' what you are 'thinking' and therefore cannot respond quickly to your light aids. The same applies to the leg aid. In the early exercises, as soon as the horse gave the required response to the button the leg aid was removed but now it is time to progress to leaving a light, feeling leg aid *in situ* to act as a 'telephone line' from your body to his.

HOW SHOULD IT FEEL? Like a partnership with each feeling and understanding the other's requests and resistances and giving appropriate educated responses.

GOAL: To have a confident forward-going horse with a soft mouth giving a consistent and easy feel on the rein and the leg, at all speeds.

PITFALLS: Beware of horses falling behind the bit or the leg, or running away from the aids: light can easily become too light and develop into avoidance. Ensure there is always a soft but positive feel between you and your horse.

DON'T LOSE HEART
There are three stages in learning to ride well:
*When the rider is very tired and the horse not at all
*When both horse and rider are tired
*Finally, when the horse is tired and the rider not at all – that is the goal!

JP and Syd working well into the contact in canter travers, ready to go into the main arena

CAN YOUR HORSE… stay soft and forward through upward and downward transitions, maintaining a fluent contact on the hand and leg.

LONG-TERM BENEFITS: To have a horse that is easy to communicate with, not seeking to push through nor drop behind the aids at any time but happy to maintain a contact and follow the feel, in hand or ridden.

Daisy and Flo following the feel and maintaining contact

Exercise 15: Achieving direct flexion at the poll

Why? Training a horse to flex at the poll, his axis, and remain soft in the jaw and, therefore, in your hand allows the energy from his hindquarters to be softly contained within his body, giving the rider easy control of his impulsion through the bit. He will be able to carry his poll high, face vertical and neck long and, once he engages behind adequately, lift his shoulders. Flexing in the neck is to be avoided as this causes overbending and is an evasion.

How? IN HAND: Start with a square balanced halt then ask the horse to bring some energy into your hand: using your stick carefully at the go button on the girth and holding the halter or bit in your hand, ask the horse to come forward into the contact, block any forward movement at the stop button with the hand and await flexion at the poll so that his face becomes vertical. The instant he gives even a tiny flex, release the pressure on his head, reward with a rub and then repeat, repeat, repeat. Beware he doesn't only move his feet back or

⬆ One of the many ways to ask for direct flexion is pressure on the nose. Roger is asking Whisky to yield flex at the poll. He keeps asking until she yields then rewards her with a nice rub on the head

just bend or flex his neck instead of flexing at the poll. (Please note that the aids for rein back are similar but should feel slightly different to the horse, with the rider's body language inviting and encouraging him to step back.) If your horse is finding flexing difficult, teach a basic flex button on his nose by pressing a fingernail into his nose bone under the noseband, releasing it the moment he flexes. Progress to asking for the same flexion from pressure on the halter noseband.

JUMPING NOTE

It is important that all horses can see where they are going, but even more vital when jumping. Be sure your horse's eyes are looking forward, not at his feet. Encourage him to look at and assess each jump from as far away as possible, so that you can work out between you how best to jump it. Good forward planning is good leadership.

⬇ Joanna asks for direct flexion using pressure on the nose ...

⬇ ... before progressing to asking for a yield off the bit.

⬆ 1) Hannah uses her leg and blocks forward movement to ask for direct flexion; 2) At first she gets too much of a response as the horse bends his neck too; 3) But on the next try, they get it right

RIDDEN: In the halt ask the horse for a little forward energy to come up to his bridle and then, instead of allowing him to move his feet or bend his neck, ask him to flex his poll through pressure on the bit, the stop button in the mouth. Allow what is right and block what is not right. Reward any attempt at the right response and then repeat, repeat, repeat.

You can move on to doing this work in the walk, trot and canter when you are both ready. He should be happy to maintain a contact – when he flexes at the poll, follow the feel, keeping a soft contact with the mouth, and ask him to remain in that soft rein contact throughout his work. If he overbends or drops the contact, he has also dropped behind the leg, so ask and allow him to come up in front of the leg again.

HOW SHOULD IT FEEL? Soft and light – not forced. The horse's jaw should be relaxed and his body and mind in harmony softly seeking the contact with the bit and your hand, with no desire to push against it.

GOAL: To have a horse that will bring his energy from his hindquarters into the contact of your hand and remain soft in the jaw and flex at the poll while maintaining high levels of energy.

PITFALLS: If the horse is flexed at the poll his peripheral vision is reduced – although he can still see ahead – therefore, it is the rider's obligation to look up and around so that the horse feels safe that he will be warned of any approaching danger. If he's worrying about any 'tigers' sneaking up on him, he may resist the rider and raise his head. Overbending, when he flexes at the poll and in his neck as well, is worse as by evading contact he avoids control of his head. Draw reins are the worst gadget for encouraging this fault to develop.

CAN YOUR HORSE… flex at the poll without overbending to look good for a photograph?

LONG-TERM BENEFITS: This will help to achieve good competition results, with the poll as the highest point, and good neck carriage.

⬇ Direct flexion will be willingly given in reponse to the riders 'ask' by a horse that is working in self carriage and going sofltly forward into the contact, it should not be forced.

⬇ A horse should be encouraged to focus ahead when jumping.

Exercise 16: Working in harmony and being 'on the bit'

Why? Once a horse is truly balanced, working with impulsion within a rounded frame and has been educated to give light responses to the aids, he can be described as being on the bit, or more literally 'on the aids'. This makes him balanced, easy to ride and able to perform complicated movements with ease. The term is misleading as a balanced educated horse has no real need of a bit. When he is truly on the aids, most signals are given by the rider's body statement, or position, and the legs; the bit sits in a soft jaw and just keeps the flexion at the poll and controls the flow of energy out of the forehand by allowing what is right and blocking what is wrong. When requests are made via the buttons, the horse is willing and able to respond to them easily and happily.

▷ When a horse is 'on the bit' he is balanced over all four feet and in harmony with his rider

▽ In hand work in walk and trot is very helpful. Here Joanna's left hand is too low, but The Colt is trotting forward well despite this

How? IN HAND: Use a halter or bridle and work facing him so you will be walking backwards or sideways aligning your body accurately and pointing your centre with care. With your left hand, hold both the reins (or the rope) with equal feel under his chin and hold your stick in your right hand (as you progress you can put the reins/rope over his neck and have your hands by his shoulder); if you prefer you can use the stick and one rein in your right hand. The stick is a substitute for your legs and needs to be quite light and just the right length to touch the three buttons on his flank (see exercise 11). Use the stick to ask for impulsion

ARE YOU READY FOR WORK ON THE BIT?

Working a horse on the bit in hand or ridden is a complex skill, so *you* may need tuition before you can achieve it. Learn on a schoolmaster if you have not worked at this level before. Once the horse is confident in his responses in the earlier exercises, ask him for more engagement and energy from behind. In order for your horse to give you total control of his body, he needs to be confident in your trustworthiness as his selected leader – your skills need to be adequate to ask for and receive this. Much has been said about this already but it is the vital key to a successful partnership.

◁ Pippa Funnell and Primmore's Pride working in harmony

and to control his body just as you would with your leg. Use your hand to control the energy. From here, with adequate forward planning and energy, you can practise or perform any movement you like. All transitions and halts, all turns, shoulder in and leg yielding can all be wonderful done like this.

RIDDEN: Prepare your horse by revising all the different buttons and once he is truly balanced and offering soft, forward, supple, resistance-free work then that's it – he is on the bit – enjoy!

HOW SHOULD IT FEEL? A little like walking on a tightrope because, until you become accomplished and accustomed to riding a horse on the bit you will be fearful of losing that perfect feeling of balance and harmony. Focus on maintaining all the different ingredients and remember a horse cannot respond to two buttons used at the same moment, but can respond when they are used in quick succession.

GOAL: A balanced, supple horse going softly forward on the aids at all times.

PITFALLS: If you are seeking further engagement of the hocks, or collection for passage or piaffe, you may find *some* experts suggest a longer training stick. However, I believe that the extra engagement should come from an ask on the go button behind the girth where the rider's leg can act, not from smacking the haunches or pressure behind the tail. If you have to rely on a training stick, the horse is not truly offering himself to you and an ugly element of force comes in, which is not good leadership and will affect your relationship with him (see 'Choosing a Trainer', above).

⬆ Soft, forward and straight – on the bit. Daisy and Gregory are progressing well

CAN YOUR HORSE... remain in partnership and harmony with you?

LONG-TERM BENEFITS: The world is your oyster. Realize your horse's maximum potential!

Exercise 17: Galloping and remaining gentle at speed

Why? It is important to be able to control your horse's feet at any speed, in any direction, at any time – this is what makes him a safe, rideable, fearless horse. Galloping is an area of ridden training most riders avoid, expecting to have to hang on for dear life and grin and bear it if the horse pulls. However, if he has progressed up through the Effective Training exercises and has understood his stop button and learned to remain gentle and respectful of his rider's aids then this is simply the next stage of his development. After their legs have been hardened up with slow work on firm ground, even young horses can do some canter work around a field every few days when the going is good; you can also do canter work in an arena.

How? RIDDEN: Settle your horse in walk and trot, moving his feet and asking him to remain soft by doing lots of bending, downwards transitions and halts. When he is calm, obedient and confident, begin cantering in a 20m (65ft) circle, only introducing straight lines when you are sure that you can flex him and keep him gentle at any time. I recommend that, in the first instance, this schooling is done with the horse working alone as he needs to find his own natural rhythm and speed, without the distraction of a companion. If he starts to brace or pull at you, use the lateral flexion button to ask for bend and softness. If necessary, turn him in small circles until he comes gentle again. Practise and establish your galloping or jumping position, standing up out of the saddle, while working in slow paces before you try going faster.

Begin by riding in a slow working canter, checking that your horse can breathe easily in rhythm with his feet, then simply ask him to go to and fro from working canter into medium canter and back – always keeping the same tempo and ensuring it is soft and easy – gradually maintaining the medium canter for longer. Ask him to work into a following but fairly strong contact as he will need a little support for his balance, which you can help him with, but don't over-support him or hold him up.

Only when medium is easy, go for few strides extended and back to medium and repeat calmly as before. Include plenty of bending, transitions and changes of direction. To maintain your concentration, focus on objects in the distance to get straight lines, and circle a thistle plant, for example, to get good round circles; when you are focused, your horse will be too. It may take you several sessions to get this far, that's ok!

Next you can allow the extended canter to level out and become a gallop for a few strides. The difference is in the balance, the extended canter being much more uphill than the gallop, and the leg sequence, which goes from three time to four time. Horses need to lower their head and come more onto their forehand to gallop well, but this should not be an excuse for them to pull on you or for you to carry them in your hands. They should still lift their back and engage their quarters, especially in downward transitions. Working on moving up and down the gears within the pace is wonderful training for both of you, and stretching out is so good for your horse and your soul.

BREATHING

You can learn a lot by listening to a horse breathing as he works.

*Healthy horses breath in rhythm with their legs, so when their legs are working in a steady rhythm so are their lungs.

*Some anxious horses hold their breath, so when a horse is breathing easily and regularly you know he is probably calm.

◁ Roger and The Colt enjoy a gallop (far left); Greg and Whiskers and Roger and The Colt canter beside each other, not racing, but remaining polite and gentle with each other and their riders (left)

⤒ Leapfrog training – one horse and rider pair canters past the other pair then halts. The other pair then does the same

⤒ One horse waits while the other works – teaching patience

HOW SHOULD IT FEEL? This is when you really feel the benefit of all your groundwork training – a balanced, safe, rideable gallop – heaven!

GOAL: To have your horse remain gentle and rideable at ever increasing levels of energy and speed, and become a delight to ride anywhere.

PITFALLS: Don't exhaust your horse – plan your progress using good leadership skills. Avoid straight lines initially, as the horse can more easily lock onto both reins and engage both hocks and push at you. If he does do this, remember to use lateral flexion and, if necessary, turn him onto a circle and even leg yield until he learns to relax and settle at that pace, only allowing straight lines when he is gentle again. Even cantering can become dull, so watch out for tedium encouraging resistances – go somewhere different or work with another horse. You can practise cantering upsides or going the opposite way, play games of leapfrog (overtaking each other and circling back), practise hunter trial courses with or without the jumps, use your imagination and invent scenarios that represent real life.

CAN YOUR HORSE… canter in front of and behind others softly, confidently and under control, and stand still while others gallop?

LONG-TERM BENEFITS: Imagine being able to go through all the gears softly and easily from working canter to full gallop, alone or in company, and walk or stand still whenever you like – the perfect trainer's hack!

HOW TO RIDE AT THE GALLOP

Learn to develop an independent seat and well-balanced position with a still leg, a following hand with a perpendicular upper arm and an easy body position that remains off the horse's back without clinging onto the reins or the neck. We always use neckstraps so never risk losing our balance. Never go flat-out with reins flapping because if the horse stumbles you will all go a purler. You can bridge the reins if necessary, but beware of the horse leaning on you, or you on him.

⤒ Even the very best riders use neckstraps – William Fox-Pitt on Tamarillo (Badminton 2004)

Exercise 17

Exercise 18: Straightness and developing focus for jumping skinnies

Why? Straightness in the horse is essential for both dressage and jumping and is not that easy to achieve. You will need to use all the buttons you have carefully cultivated to be able to correct any unwanted wobbles and bends. This is also an opportunity to have some fun putting into practice all the previous training you have done and seeing how accurately you can ride. Remember it is you who is the leader and should move the horse's feet; working in accurate straight lines consolidates this and gains still more respect from the horse.

How? IN HAND AND RIDDEN: Set out some poles, cones and tubs, making narrow places to pass through, 'tunnels' to travel along and awkward turns to negotiate. Begin by riding, leading or lunging through them in the slow paces and build up to higher speeds, always including transitions to check your gears and buttons are working well. Use the lateral flexion buttons to keep him straight and soft, and to prevent him spooking.

Once you are both confident and competent on the flat, begin to include some jumps or hazards. Use your focus to have your horse stay on-line; check your horse's focus by placing jackets on the fence to try to distract him. Increase your accuracy by placing peppermints on the poles and jumping between them – share them with him afterwards.

◁ Roger and Whiskers developing straightness by working through narrow spaces

▽ Joanna rides Windy 'down a tunnel' between hand and leg to achieve straightness

HOW SHOULD IT FEEL? Like riding through a tunnel, or being on an arrow!

GOAL: To be able to keep your line with your horse continuing to focus, whatever happens around the arena or course.

PITFALLS: Your horse might seek to go flat or level when asked to go straight and may fall on his forehand. He will need extra help to remain engaged

◁ The Colt stays straight to jump the centre barrel

behind and rounded in his back when working straight. Remember to ride from the back to the front: think of him as a unicorn and keep that head straight ahead by using your legs on the buttons to prevent any deviation, or to bend him if he gets strong or rude.

CAN YOUR HORSE… keep doing his job even when a friend tries to distract him by moving around, playing football or throwing things across in front of you?

LONG-TERM BENEFITS: This is an important area of training that often gets omitted and yet is vital for safety and excellent work for the competition horse, which has to work well in straight lines and endure endless distractions.

⬆ Daisy asks Flo not to look at the jump but to focus straight ahead

⬇ Sophie asks Charlie to stay straight and jump this skinny. Thank you

⬇ Straightness is required to fly Vicarage Vee at Badminton. Pippa Funnell and Primmore's Pride show how it's done

Exercise 19: Working in – showground and collecting ring strategies

⤒ Accustom your horses to living by the lorry before going to shows

Why? The true purpose of competing is to prove how good your training has been – so at a competition you want your horse's behaviour and performance to be impeccable. Every horse is different and you will need to adapt your procedures accordingly. Be aware that people at a show are not all your friends and they probably will not care if things go wrong for you. There are even people who become maniacs in the collecting ring! (Avoid ending up parked near these types by exploring the showground before you unload your horse.)

Other preparation should include working in confined spaces with other horses, and spookbusting (see Exercise 20).

◁ Roger and Joanna with The Colt and Whiskers, training them to be happy to stand away from each other

⤒ In a very busy collecting ring, Syd and JP are calm and relaxed, thanks to their previous practice, which builds on confidence for these testing situations

How? IN HAND AND RIDDEN:
Develop a working-in system that helps your horse prepare both physically and mentally for the forthcoming challenge. In addition, keep your wits about you, plan ahead and know your job, this will give your horse confidence in your leadership and he will be less worried.

At the competition, try not to be vague, remember to tell your horse where you want him to go and what you want him to do; he can only guess from your body signals so help him to get it right. His adrenaline will be higher than usual and he may feel threatened – he really needs your leadership now; don't abandon him because of your own anxieties. Ensure that you allow enough time to let him to have a good look around, loosen him up, move his feet a lot, then polish up ready for the ring. All the work you have done before, especially the cantering and leapfrog will help him to settle among other horses, but also do some work alone, as you will probably be alone in the arena.

Chill out together. Just going to competitions to spend time with your horse on the showground, without participating, is a vital part of any young horse's training, or retraining for a spoiled horse. Take every opportunity to teach him how to relax in the strange surroundings and atmosphere. When you arrive work him as you would to prepare him for a competition, then instead of putting him away just stay by the arena until he relaxes. Spend a happy time together watching, learning, grazing and maybe share an ice cream!

⇩ Joanna wishes JP and Syd good luck as they go into the main arena. Syd's calm demeanour is a result of good training

HOW SHOULD IT FEEL? As though all the buttons are primed and you are both ready for the competition ahead, which is well within your capabilities as a team.

GOAL: To give your horse the skills to help him to succeed in your chosen task. Make it a rewarding experience for him, too – he didn't enter the competition, you did, and he hates to fail and loves to succeed, too!

PITFALLS: Horses can bring out the worst in people, and competition nerves exacerbate this – some people become aggressive, others shut down and fail to show their horses any leadership at all. Both these scenarios make life difficult for their horse who may well choose to go home – right now, and you might be in his way! Avoid becoming either of the above by working on your own coping strategies for competition nerves and being prepared.

CAN YOUR HORSE... be the best-behaved horse at the show?

LONG-TERM BENEFITS: This work builds confidence and trust, and enables you to perform perfectly in harmony.

Exercise 20: Spookbusting – putting the finishing touches to your fearless horse

Why? Developing the fearless horse involves much training, including spookbusting, or acclimatization. It is your responsibility to prepare well and train your horse to be confident with all the different stimuli and situations he is likely to meet, especially if he going competing; crowds and clapping are the most obvious ones. This work can be good fun and is extremely good training for all people and horses.

We have developed the following spookbusting strategies partly in order to ensure our Primmore foals, which we have to sell as babies, set out into the big wide world as well equipped as possible. Primmore's Pride is a shining example of how good training as a foal can last a lifetime. He never worries at a prize-giving ceremony or in a parade and trusts his rider Pippa Funnell totally. We also use similar strategies when teaching and when training or retraining competition horses with our clients.

⇧ Joanna throws the ball and Gregory braces but Daisy is there for him to ask him to remain soft and gentle

⇧ Daisy asks Gregory to rein back between the flower tubs – a common source of shying in the arena, once adrenaline has been raised

⇧ Felicity teaches Pudding not to be fearful of toys on pillars!

REMEMBER: WHO IS TRAINING WHOM?

You are training your horse to become braver and accept our strange world. Be careful he isn't training you to keep all spooks away from him. You should be moving his feet, don't let him move yours, physically or emotionally. If, for example, he snorts and braces at the sight of an umbrella, he is telling you in no uncertain terms to take that horrid thing away from him. It is very important that you use all your training skills to keep him standing there, helping him to become gentle until he tries to accept the spook by softening and relaxing a little, then you can remove the umbrella and relax and reward him, enjoy a little soak time before repeat, repeat, repeat. If he is trying to run away from or refusing to look at the spook, you may be advancing too fast, retreat a little to a smaller spook and restart there. It is all about good judgment, goal setting, feel and timing (see pp.39 and 56–57).

YOU WILL NEED: For real spookbusting, the more noisy, spooky items you can accumulate, the better; collect them gradually. My tool box (lorry) usually contains some or all of the following: portable hi-fi for loud music, rustly tree branches, sticks with things on the end, footballs, old hats or Frisbees to throw, plastic sheeting, large cardboard boxes, several flags (homemade is fine), large space hoppers, umbrellas, a heavy tarpaulin or a heavy non-slip board. I also have a collection of old tin cans filled with pebbles to simulate clapping. It's also useful to have blocks to stack up or jump over and skinny 1m (3ft) poles to test your focus, a water tray (or paddling pool), fillers and banners to put on jumps, lots of people to help … the list is endless.

How? IN HAND AND RIDDEN: Work on the best surface available in as safe and controlled environment as possible and keep any spectators out of harm's way. Prepare your horse by going through the previous exercises until he is gentle, trusting, all buttons are primed and he is on the aids, then begin by gradually introducing the spooks and asking him to ignore them. Your judgment and timing of what to introduce when and what 'size' or speed is crucial: too much and you will scare him, too little and he will not progress. Use the advance and retreat work (pp.36–41) with him by making the chosen spook gradually bigger, closer or faster and

⇧ Gregory has progressed from footballs to spacehoppers. Thanks to careful training he is not worried at all

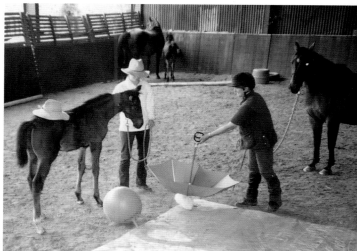

⇧ Rachel and Joanna work with Primmore's Patience who is virtually bombproof by three months old. Mother – Panache – is not so sure

◁ The Colt wants to fly his own flag!

↑ Pippa Funnell and Primmore's Pride are totally relaxed together at the Chatsworth prizegiving ceremony

Your timing and your speed of reaction to something your horse does are what teach him right from wrong. Your success depends on a good decision on when, how, how much, your consistency and rewarding only good responses. Poor training is too little or too much, too soon or too late and rewarding bad responses. Practise on willing guinea pigs, human, canine, feline, camelid, bovine, ovine or porcine, until you get good, then try this out on your old horse before your young one. Skilled handling of the training equipment is important and takes practice, too, so the same creeds apply.

as soon as he shows he is trying to accept it then retreat it to a safe distance – instantly stopping the pressure and accepting the try – relax and reward him with a little soak time before repeat, repeat, repeat in ever advancing difficulty. Keep the lesson short, 20 minutes maximum at one session, and include lots of soak times.

HOW SHOULD IT FEEL? Like you are the proud senior partner who has prepared a junior partner to cope in any situation.

GOAL: To have a fearless horse that is confident with anything the world slings at him.

PITFALLS: Some surprising and alarming results can be produced from seemingly quiet horses and with small spooks, and you need to be aware of what the horse is telling you and how to keep yourself safe. Sometimes a horse will seem to be accepting

a spooky object but after a few minutes will decide to take fright. This is another way of asking you to take the spook away, which, of course, you won't do until he becomes gentle again…he is just checking who is the leader! Watch out that you are not progressing too fast or standing too close, making him worried. He will tell you through excessive licking and chewing, becoming bargy or shutting down. Learn to read the signs (see 'Listen to Your Horse', box, p.14) and revise the buttons and exercises as necessary before you proceed.

CAN YOUR HORSE… carry the flag at the next Olympic Games?

LONG-TERM BENEFITS: This will give you a bombproof horse, and educate him in as many diverse situations as possible. You should end up with a wonderful 'horse of a lifetime' – a versatile, rideable, enjoyable and fearless horse.

⇧ Rachel focuses straight ahead, giving Buddy confidence going through a narrow gap beside our poster (top); Passion is looking worried by the spooks and pushes towards Joanna. More schooling is needed and we progress in small steps until she is more confident (above)

OUR BEST FEARLESS HORSE

Primmore Hill our founder mare, was bought as a foal in 1973. She became so versatile she would do all the stock work on the farm, tow the local children on toboggans when it snowed, take an adult and a child to meet the school bus – often carrying a large musical instrument too – lead all the children's ponies and young horses, train children in the local Pony Club, wait patiently tied to the back door while I answered the telephone and even share her stable with sick calves, licking them back to health. She could also win dressage and show jumping competitions, carry the farmer out hunting – over big hedges or up on rough moors – gallop with young racehorses and complete the course at Badminton with the fastest time over the fiercest fences – finishing ninth. And then she bred five foals, each a star and one a world-beating champion, Primmore's Pride – her life was never dull and she was our horse of a lifetime! Her progeny now follow in her footsteps…

⇧ Primmore Hill aged 23, a face full of generosity and courage

◁ Primmore Hill takes Nicky Stephens boldly clear around their first Badminton in 1982

113

TROUBLESHOOTING
AND REMEDIAL SCHOOLING

Most difficulties in the horse–human relationship arise from the human's poor leadership or unrealistic expectations of the horse. Horses love to follow a strong and caring leader and, being naturally totally honest, unbelievably tolerant and generous, make great junior partners. Most horse behaviours we consider problems are the horse's attempts to check on our leadership or draw our attention to his anxieties, pain or fear. Horses cannot reason, therefore they cannot plot to be troublesome – even though they have superb memories, they live in the present, that is NOW! If your horse becomes 'difficult', adopt a holistic approach to discover what is at the heart of the problem.

Before you get tough with him – ask yourself how he will benefit from complying with your requests. Is he being troublesome because he is uneducated or confused, or is he uncomfortable? Use your intelligence and leadership to analyze the situation and with the help of the advice, schooling exercises and strategies in this book, you will find an easier way forward.

Before you consider yourself ready to try to cope with or solve any problems you need – at least – to understand the training methods and strategies described in this book. Also ensure you have prepared yourself and your horse thoroughly for this work, either from the ground or ridden, by going through the relevant exercises in section 2 (see list right). You may find your troubles will dissolve along the way. Troubleshooting is a huge subject, so we have only included a few of the most common problems that we meet. However, as you will see, they are all improved by using similar strategies – employing an understanding approach, good leadership, good schooling and good training to develop a trusting partnership.

This section is divided into the difficulties you might encounter at the stable yard (pp.116–126), when riding (pp.127–143) and those that you might meet in competition situations (pp.144–149).

THE EXERCISES

Before you start troubleshooting, check through the list of exercises below – there may be one you want to try first.

⬆ With horses, troubleshooting is more about understanding and retraining yourself and your horse than finding a quick fix for your problem

At the yard

Many common problems that occur at yards could be avoided with some improved practices and good routines that everyone follows and understands. Use the Effective Training exercises to prevent these problems occurring.

• Headshyness

Horses instinctively know they should keep their head free and safe from predators, so it takes training and time for them to feel confident to entrust you with it. Unfortunately, humans always go to the head first: we hug and kiss each other in greeting, or throttle our enemies and slit the throat of our prey. The horse knows this, so don't blame him for his fears when you try to control him by his head.

Use advance and retreat techniques and exercises 2, 4 and 14 to help overcome headshyness. Progress as follows, in easy stages over several sessions, making sure he accepts each stage before moving on:

• Ask yourself what's in it for him? And see if an improved approach to the issue works. During this work, be careful not to reward the wrong behaviour by stopping what you are doing too soon (see 'Who is Training Whom?', p.40).

• Rub him gently with a soft cloth and work at gradually moving towards his head.

• Ask him to accept your hand placed on his head and gently start to move his head around.

• Use a halter and by using pressure and release (see p.36) train him to hold his head low and confidently, while you rub his poll. (Never use a pressure halter with uncomfortable fittings on the headpiece that press into the poll.)

• Yield his head up and down and from side to side.

• Start moving objects around his head and placing things progressively closer to it.

• Hang safe things in his stable, construct toys that he has to push under or through and take him out to the woods and ask him to push through trees and branches.

⇨ Roger is teaching Whisky how to yield her head down. At first she braces but through pressure and release she eventually becomes much softer in her attempts. Timing is the key with this work. The slightest yield or lessening of resistance must be rewarded instantly with a 'yes' release of pressure to encourage the horse to seek the release again

GREETING AND CATCHING

Think how horses greet each other by touching outstretched noses, and offer him the back of your outstretched hand to be sniffed first (easier and safer than offering your nose!). Touch his shoulder, explain that you mean no harm, then politely place the headcollar on his head; avoid grabbing him and dragging his head into your space and buckling on a cold wet headcollar.

◁ Passion shows how easy it is, yielding to pressure on the leadrope – this skill is very useful if the horse accidentally steps on the leadrope or gets caught on something

• Use a cordless hairdryer to 'touch' his ears. Begin with gentle warm air if he is very shy (hold the hairdryer quite a way away at first). If he jumps, keep it running until he relaxes, then reward him for trying to relax by taking the hairdryer away (retreating). Be careful not to reward the wrong behaviour by taking it away too soon (see 'Who is Training Whom?' p. 40).

• Get him leading really well and working in hand (see exercise 8). Only when he is good with all this, probably after several sessions, should you progress to tying up (see overleaf).

AN HOLISTIC APPROACH

Headshyness can be an indication of pain, so as soon as you have gained the horse's confidence, have his feet, back, neck and teeth checked. Choose your therapist carefully and be sure they understand his worries and don't hurt him further.

▷ Passion accepts toys on her head! I'm not forcing her to stay – the leadrope is quite slack, but if she chose to go I would ask her to come back and continue with the training until staying becomes her decision

• Pulling back when tied up

Once a horse is successful at breaking away when tied up and, therefore, achieves his goal of escaping captivity, pulling back can become a habit. The piece of his education that is missing is the knowledge that he has nothing to fear, and that yielding and moving his feet will release pressure on his head. The worst thing you can do to cure pulling back is to tie him to an immovable object and let him fight it out. You will probably end up with a dead or injured horse. Instead teach him pressure and release by going through exercises 1–9 and then concentrating on the rein back to move forward; this is also useful when the horse's knees become locked and he forgets how to move forward. Practise this until it is foolproof before starting work on tying up. (See also Pulling Away, opposite.)

Begin tying up practice by pretending you are the ring to which the horse is tied and have him move his feet, walking from one side to the other and then to and fro, backwards and forwards. Next slip the rope through the ring, but hold the end in your hand, rather than tying it, and move him around as before. Then tie him to an old inner-tube, bungee tie, or string that will break if he panics and repeat again. Make sure that he is soft in all this work; if he shows signs of bracing, return to the exercises. Repeat this work every day until he is totally confident moving on his tie and being left there while life goes on all around him.

▷ I'm moving this young mare from side to side and forwards and backwards so that she learns that she can release pressure from the headcollar by moving her feet, staying gentle and not bracing

⬇ Gregory a seasoned competition horse, teaches young Flo to be quite happy to stand tied to the 'wagon'

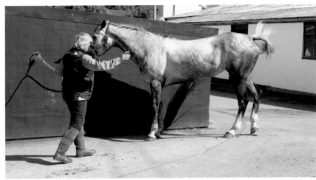

• Pulling away

Pulling away or refusing to move while being led is a very common resistance. It is particularly dangerous if the handler is using the standard 2m (6ft) lead rope. She tries to pull the horse forward towards her, and the horse resists by pulling back into a little rear, which drags the handler towards him, then the horse leaps into the air towards the handler, aiming with a shoulder or striking with a front leg. The handler has to leap out of the way as the horse gallops past and off into the distance. This is not vicious or unusual behaviour; if you think about what happened here, you will find that the horse had no choice. Where else could he go? He felt threatened by the handler pulling him against his will and he needed to escape in the quickest and most effective way. Think of yourself being pulled towards someone you don't quite trust – you would fight and break free too. Every horse has the ability to save himself from situations he considers threatening, and his strong survival-of-the-fittest instincts kick in once he feels unsafe.

When leading any horse, be careful that you are not unintentionally pulling him into you – send him out to an arm's length away if he is too close. Flick a loop along the rope towards him to send him back out of your space or send him out on a circle (see exercises 1, 9 and 13).

⇨ 1) Whiskers puts her tongue over her bit, which makes her panic and pull back

2) She tries to pull away but Jemima stays with her asking her to wait, think and not try to flee

3) Jemima works on calming Whiskers by moving her feet, circling her around

4) Gradually Jemima restores the situation and regains her role as trusted leader, and can now quietly sort out the bridle

• Exercising and grazing in hand

Exercising a horse in hand, especially one that has been cooped up on box rest for some weeks, can be stressful. Do plenty of Effective Training in the stables, using exercises 1 to 9, before venturing out. It is best to use a training halter or bridle with a long lead rope, and carry a stiff stick to help you to block him if he gets too keen. If you are leading in a paddock make sure you set off with a plan and go from one point to another. Do lots of transitions from halt to walk as you go and even turn and circle if this is appropriate. If you have to exercise on a public road, train him to lead well in your left hand before you set out, so that you can keep him straight and close to the verge. Set off with a great sense of purpose and have someone with you to direct the traffic for you. Use the stick in front of him to block his forward progress or to keep him straight, walking backwards if necessary (see exercise 8). If possible, keep close to a fence to make blocking easier for you if he is very fresh.

⇧ Snatching a quick snack is one of the disadvantages of schooling on grass. Tap his nose or shake the rope to retrieve his attention

⇧ Roger schools Charlie to halt when he does by using a strong upright blocking body statement into the halt

⇧ Despite temptation, your horse can be taught not to grab for food. The Colt shows off his good manners to our well supervised little helper

◁ Roger carries a stick to use as an extension of his left arm if The Colt is lazy or to block him if he starts to pull. Knotted halters or a Dually are useful for this work until the horse has learned to be respectful

◁ Jaz finds it difficult to lift Pudding's head. Effective Training would teach the pony to be more respectful and Jaz to be more successful, but she is trying hard under our watchful eye

▽ 1 and 2) The instant Passion lowers her head to eat, Roger sends a loop down the rope to bump her face and wriggle her headcollar annoyingly

3) He continues this until Passion raises her head and decides it is easier not to snatch at the grass, a decision that is rewarded by stillness in the rope

As you walk, the horse may try to snatch at grass, so you need to have a rule that he never grazes unless halted and invited to by you. School him through exercises 1 to 9 to develop a more respectful relationship. When you intend to allow him to graze, set out with purpose and when you reach the grazing area halt him and when he is standing politely invite him to lower his head and eat. Interrupt him from time to time and ask him to lift his head and move on – this confirms that you are controlling his feet. Never let him drag you about. If he is snatching at grass, school him by immediately flicking a loop along the rope to bump him on the nose or tap his nose or go button with your stick at the split second that he snatches. Your timing needs to be accurate; don't pull at him because you will be too slow and will only pull him into your space. If he persistently snatches, have him halt and stand and not graze (which is hard for him) and only when that schooling is established allow him to graze again. If you (and all his handlers) are consistent and fair it won't take very long for him to learn the rules.

◁ The Colt sets a perfect example with Joanna's grandson Aaron

• **Biting kicking and aggressive behaviour**

These are all expressions of mental or physical discomfort, offence at your actions, defensiveness or possibly lack of respect. By working through the Effective Training exercises you will overcome most of these issues.

Nipping can be a tricky habit to cure but perseverance with no tidbits or hand feeding at all, and consistency with everyone involved with the horse, will succeed. Ask everyone to 'keep out of his face' and not to allow him to put his head into their space or to touch them with his nose (see exercises 1–5). Try to anticipate when he will nip and, as he does, catch his muzzle on a bony bit of your body, so that he thinks 'Oops, that was uncomfortable – won't do that again!' This self-inflicted discomfort is by far the best training aid. Allow him to experience it every time he tries to nip.

Kicking is usually improved after working through the Effective Training exercises and schooling the horse to accept movement around his hind end (see particularly exercises 2–7).

Aggression also will usually dissipate once you begin to use your leadership and body language better and work through the exercises. Feed time bullying, for example, can be reduced by moving the horse around and sending him back (see exercises 1–7) while you place the feed in the bin; while horses that hog the manger can be discouraged from doing so by practising in an open space and asking the horse to yield step by step sideways around his feed tub while eating, see exercise 11. Once he realizes he can move and not lose his food then he will become less protective.

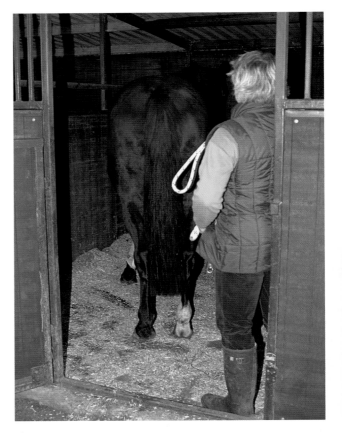

⇧ If a horse turns his quarters to you, swing a rope annoyingly across your body to put pressure on him to turn around and face you. When he does, stop swinging the rope and draw his head to you. Take care not to get too close to his back legs

HEADSHAKING

Headshaking is not a 'vice', nor an attempt to avoid work. It is usually a neurological problem or an allergy to insects or sunlight; it is most common in warm weather and may be related to the heat dilating the facial blood vessels and nerve channels. Sometimes it is based on a pelvic or saddle problem and we find acupressure or McTimoney chiropractic highly effective at alleviating the symptoms. Consult an expert as there are many different ways to relieve the problem, which can be as painful as facial neuralgia in humans.

• **Reluctant to lift feet or farrier shy**

Horses that worry about the farrier have often had bad experiences and need considerate retraining. As far as the farrier is concerned, he has a lot of horses to shoe in a day and doesn't want to be hauled about or delayed; as far as the horse is concerned, he is not going to allow just anyone to hold his feet, and bang nails into them unless he is sure they mean him no harm.

It is your responsibility to train your horse for the farrier, and to show good leadership by helping your horse to understand what is going to happen, when and how. Would you let a stranger grab your foot and hold it up while attaching things to it? You'd certainly think 'Who are you? What do you think you are doing?' No doubt your horse feels the same way too. Prepare the horse by gaining his trust and showing that by giving you his foot he is not endangering his life, which is what his instincts tell him. He knows his feet are his best chance of escape and without them he is dead.

Teach him to accept shoeing in stages. Teach him to remain gentle while:
• Standing still unaided
• Standing on three legs for gradually increasing lengths of time – you can train this by asking him to stand with one foot up on a block
• Allowing each of his feet to be held up a little bit (see box, right)
• Allowing each of his feet to be held up in a light then tighter clasp
• Allowing each of his legs to be manoeuvered into shoeing positions
• Having his feet rasped and tapped
• Having his feet banged with a steel hammer

• Accepting the noise of steel hitting steel on his foot
• Accepting smoke coming from his own foot
• Accepting having someone (usually a big man) leaning into his belly
• Accepting having someone moving quickly around close to him and grabbing and dropping noisy tools (see exercises 4 and 5).

Now he is 'gentle' and ready for the farrier.

To do this work, use a halter with a rope long enough for you to be able to reach the hind feet with plenty of rope left in your hand. Some horses take weeks to learn all this, some just minutes. You must judge how fast you can go. Practise well before the farrier arrives and have a few dress rehearsals, especially if 'strange' horses will arrive to see the farrier too; disrupting the usual routine can be worrying for an anxious horse. Avoid using tidbits to persuade him to stay still, use exercises 1–5, and pressure and release instead. Make the right thing – standing still – easy, and the wrong thing – fidgeting – difficult.

⬆ This foal is confident and working hard to keep her balance for the farrier Paul Dunning. Allowing for her inexperience he will put her foot down every few minutes, which will increase her confidence considerably

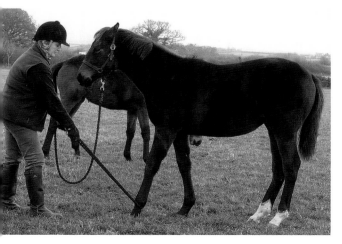

⬆ This Primmore foal is learning to balance and yield to a rope around the pastern. I'm asking her to rock her foot onto her toe, not to lift her leg, but to balance on her three other feet

FOOT TIPS

*When training, always hold the lead rope in your hand, don't tie the horse up because you can't school him by moving him around if he starts to try to move *you* around. Hold the rope in the hand nearest to the horse so if a crisis occurs you can get away from him and turn his head towards you. (If the rope is in your outside hand, you will get pulled into the horse.)

*If your horse is very worried about having his feet touched or lifted, check his back and pelvis. If these are not a problem, begin his training using a soft floor mop or feather duster to accustom him to having them touched. Next, stand him up square and using the back of the head of a house broom on the outside of his leg, slip it in behind his pastern and rock the foot onto the toe until he takes his weight off it, then quietly remove the broom and allow him to put his foot back. Always start by just asking him to rock the foot onto the toe rather than lift it right up, gradually gaining his trust before asking him to lift the foot fully.

*Always replace your horse's foot on the ground. Don't just drop it because that is unbalancing, disrespectful and can also hurt sore backs. Ask your farrier to do the same.

*Moving is not acceptable and can be discouraged with pressure applied in the form of shaking the rope and 'bumping' the halter on his head; staying still is good and rewarded with a loose rein and good scratch and rub. If you have trouble getting your horse to stand, move him around a lot then offer him the chance to stand and rest, rewarding him with a scratch and a rub.

• Scared of the vet

Vets are busy people, often with a hectic schedule to get through and this means they can be a little impatient, forgetting to greet the horse politely before examining him, which can lead to objections. Some horses are wary of strangers and the vet is just another stranger to dislike, especially as he or she often does unpleasant things, like vaccinating or tooth rasping, and may smell odd, too.

Fear of the vet is preventable, and resolvable, through the Effective Training exercises, especially 4 and 5, and use of advance and retreat to prepare for specific issues. Ask your vet to pause briefly to stroke the youngsters during visits to the yard and to move quietly and positively around your horses. For routine vaccinations, be assertive and ask the vet not to charge into the stable, bang in the needle and charge out. Ask him or her to touch and massage the injection site before and after injecting and not just to jab and jump out of the way! You are paying the vet, so don't be shy, but do thank them for their co-operation!

If the treatment is uncomfortable, you will need to reschool and reassure the horse after each visit. You could ask a friend to dress up as a vet if your horse develops a fear and even use surgical spirit to make them smell like a vet. Then just have them groom the horse sympathetically. It is good training to prepare the horse to accept a range of veterinary treatments: foot poulticing (we use babies' disposable nappies taped on with wide black tape), pretend injections, stethoscopes, teeth rasps, hosing, bathing, bandages, overhead x-ray cameras (using a cardboard box on a pole) and even standing in cross ties, in a horse spa and on a weighbridge. Use anything suitable you can think of whenever you get the chance – one day your horse may need treatment or hospitalization and you will be glad you practised. Once you have begun this way of thinking, you will never be short of things to do to improve your horse. Keep a list for inspiration on rainy days.

If your horse is going to a veterinary hospital take some familiar things with him; even a bucket of manure – his own or a friends' – can be hugely reassuring. The sterile stables might be cold so take warm rugs, nothing is worse than having to wear hospital pyjamas!

⇨ Nerve blocking The Colt is done with care and consideration by our vet Andrew Walker. The Colt's training enables him to stay calm during this invasive treatment. (He wears nylon insoles to prevent bruising)

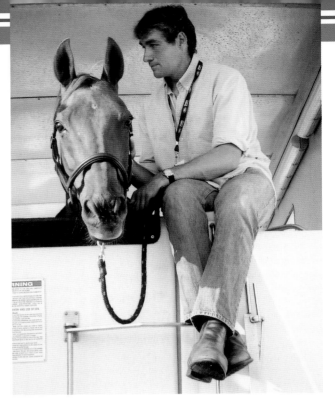

⬆ Syd relaxes in the horse spa lorry at Burghley, kept company by his rider JP Daker. Earlier this trusting partnership had completed a safe, fast clear round of the fearsome cross country course

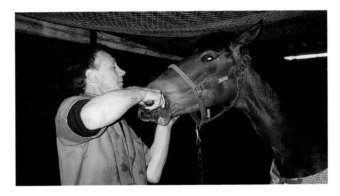

⬆ Peter Nott rasps Passion's teeth sympathetically and although she obviously dislikes the procedure they are both calm and working in harmony. The netting on the stable ceiling is a great way of preventing bumped heads

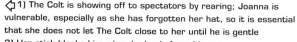 1) The Colt is showing off to spectators by rearing; Joanna is vulnerable, especially as she has forgotten her hat, so it is essential that she does not let The Colt close to her until he is gentle
2) Her stick blocks him when he lands from his rear
3) Joanna moves out to the side to send him on a circle; her stick blocks him and she shakes the rope to prevent him from coming too near. Joanna should be wearing a hard hat – lunging can be challenging
4) The Colt softens and the pair enjoys a few moments soak time
5) Now down to some good work with The Colt gentle and respectful

• Rearing and plunging in hand

Some horses will rear and then jump at you if they feel you are threatening their safety or if you are asking them to do something they don't want to do, such as loading into a trailer. Avoid getting into such situations unless you are very confident of being able to cope, and always consider your own safety never put yourself in danger. By working through the Effective Training exercises you will dissipate any of these issues, but exercises 1–5 will help especially.

• Always use a long lead rope (see pp.30 and 119) to avoid being pulled under the horse. And wear gloves, boots and a hard hat.

• Stand out to one side ready to unbalance him and disengage his quarters.

• If the horse rears and plunges, send him away firmly and allow the rope to slip through your hands as you brace your feet and belly, ready to stand firm when he hits the end and to spin him round to face you, making his escape attempt futile and uncomfortable.

• Send him around you in a small circle to avoid him barging into you. You can keep him circling for as long as you need to. Use your body language and your tools to keep him away and have his feet move in the direction you ask, not vice versa. Once he is calm, stop him politely and review your situation. You need to teach him to respect your space, understand your body signals, and trust your leadership more (work through the exercises 1–3, 8, 12 and 13).

• Lunging difficulties

If your horse tends to charge off on the lunge, reschool him by working through the Effective Training exercises, particularly 1–3, 8, 12 and 13. Only once he can do a small circle calmly, gently, softly flexed, banana-shaped and *fully* under control should you progress onto a big circle. Every time he tries to hurry, re-educate him to slow down by jerking the rope, which makes the halter bump him on the nose. You can also put your stick in front of his chest or even his head, especially if he is beside a wall, to stop him. (Make sure he is gentle to your tools, see exercises 4 and 5.) Release all pressure when he slows and reward him with a rest, even if he has been challenging your leadership skills, remain emotionally aloof and hold no grudges. Keep sessions short and sweet.

One reason why a horse becomes difficult when lunged in the traditional way is sheer boredom and frustration at the length of time he is expected to circle around with no leadership or interaction from his trainer. Any rudeness that goes uncorrected, like cutting in or pushing his ribs at you, is considered by the horse to be a sign of weak leadership and a signal that he should take charge again. Someone has to be the leader and if you aren't, he will be.

When lunging always wear a hard hat, gloves and boots.

⬆ The Colt is fresh and rudely tries to gallop off

⬆ Joanna blocks him by jerking on his head and sending his quarters out to disempower him, while blocking him from walking into her

⬆ He realizes that Joanna has the ability to move his feet at any time, speed and in any direction, and harmony is restored as he accepts her leadership

⬆ Joanna rewards The Colt for changing his mind from rough and rude to gentle and polite

Ridden work

You will find that if you have sorted out any issues on the ground using the Effective Training exercises, ridden problems will improve too. It is hardly surprising that a horse that doubts your leadership when you are on foot, may show a similar lack of respect or trust when you are in the saddle. However, you must eliminate physical discomfort as a cause for misbehaviour by checking saddle fit, back pain and all the other usual suspects before re-schooling the problem. Even if your horse is an angel to handle and only exhibits unwanted behaviour when ridden, the strategies offered in the exercises will work to improve the partnership between you, and the results you can achieve.

⬆ Daisy has four-year old Flo really well trained – she accepts any amount of movement from the person getting on

• Hard to mount

Being restless or walking off when a rider is trying to mount is usually an attempt to avoid discomfort. Remember you do not have an unquestionable right to get on a horse's back and if you do so without his full consent then he could deposit you any way he likes. Analyse the situation to see if you can discover the cause of his reluctance. It could be that you are hurting the horse as you get on, which could indicate an uncomfortable saddle, sore feet, back pain, weakness, dislike of the work required, fear of what happens next, or maybe he doesn't like being ridden.

Ensure that you move his feet and he does not move yours and do plenty of Effective Training exercises before asking him to stand by the mounting block to wait quietly while you get on. If he still seems worried get him and his saddle fit checked out before you ride again. When he stands well, pretend you are getting ready to get on, then reward him by just rubbing him instead. If he moves at all, stop rubbing, make him move his feet and then ask him to stand square and ready again, prepare to get on, reward his stillness with a rub and retreat.

Progress to pulling lightly on the pommel and rocking him to see that he is really ready, and reward him with a rub. If he is not ready, he will move off again and you should move his feet some more before asking him to stand up for you again, and repeat, repeat, repeat until he allows you to get on and off while happily standing still. When you do mount, ask him to walk in a small circle before moving off – only when he is calm. Don't let him go in a straight line until you are sure he is 'gentle'.

This work is easier with a halter and line – simply pop it on over the bridle. It is also better to work on this alone than to have someone else force him to stand. Ensure that your mounting block is away from the wall or fence so you can circle him around it, and that it is high enough for you to be able to step into the saddle, not struggle. Train your horse to be steady beside walls, gates, banks, lorry ramps and schooling blocks, and to have you receive a leg up. Make him easy to get on from anywhere. Do mounting work equally on both sides. It is good for both of you to be ambidextrous. Never mount from the ground, unless you have the ability to spring up lightly.

⬇ Roger is retraining Whiskers to be confident about being mounted anywhere – from the ground, a bank, a gate and so on

• **Bucking, broncing, rearing and spinning**
A happy healthy horse takes the line of least resistance and wants to please you, providing your leadership is good and fair. If he is prepared to fight then there has to be a cause. Listen to and watch your horse. What are his reactions when you bring his tack? If he turns his back, ask yourself is it comfortable, are you sure he is sound, are you fair and appreciative in the work you ask him to do? Even if he is fresh, he should still be gentle and respectful of you – his paddock time is his time for horseplay.

Once you are sure there is no clinical cause to his resistance, work through the Effective Training exercises, especially 1–6, and that should help a lot. Horses rear and spin to challenge your leadership or when their feet get stuck and they decide it is best to escape by fight or flight. Whether this is a learned bad behaviour or a sudden 'new' nap it is still resolved by moving the horse's feet to prevent him from successfully moving yours. Find a way to free his feet up by getting him turning, or work through exercises 2 and 7, only ask him to go straight ahead

1) Konker is rather full of himself, and although Joanna should know better she is not moving his feet enough because she is distracted by thoughts of the photoshoot (this sort of distraction so often happens at competitions); 2) She makes good use of the breastplate and manages to stay on...for a while; 3 and 4) Konker's 360-degree spin in a tenth of a second defeats her and centrifugal force wins; 5 and 6) However, she does manage to land on her feet;

7) As her falling off will have worried him, Joanna works him in hand to get him gentle and confident about her getting back on; 8 and 9) The pair recommences schooling and when Konker tries spinning again Joanna is ready to disengage his quarters to disempower him; 10) As a result he becomes gentle and respectful quite quickly and is rewarded for changing his mind and accepting her leadership politely

again once you are sure he is gentle, sometimes it is easier to proceed in half circles and loops all the way. Providing there is no clinical reason for this behaviour it will be resolved as you progress with this training approach. Avoid getting on him until you have checked how he is feeling today by moving his feet around and establishing your leadership role.

Few of us like having go to work, and the chances are your horse feels the same, but if you are sure he is not suffering, don't get soft on him. If he were living in the wild, he would have to endure even less pleasant things. Work is good for him and he has a job to do, so like the good leader that you have now become, make sure he is as fit, comfortable, healthy and well trained as possible before taking him out to do his work with you.

⬇ Konker's owner Julie continues the retraining work asking him to be gentle and accept spooky items and doing some mounting and dismounting practice.

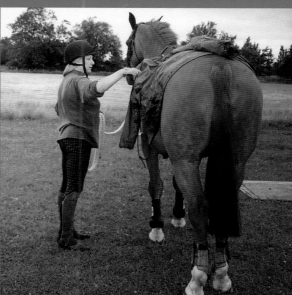

4

5

9

10

• Napping back to the lorry, stables or other horses

With napping too you need to try to work out why your horse feels the need to nap. Is it confusion, lack of confidence, fear of being on his own, or a dislike of going from the crowded working area to the lonely dressage or jumping arena?

REVIEW YOUR ATTITUDE

Could your emotions or nerves be part of the issue? Remember that in order to be a good teacher and leader, especially if you are competing or training horses or people, you do need to be mentally tough to remain detached from their and your emotions. Learn how to control your emotions before you try to influence those of others.

Perhaps the horse has a fear of pain, or remembered pain? Is it a fear of failure? If a horse is punished for getting things wrong or is not rewarded enough for getting things right, he will cease to enjoy his work and lose self-confidence. This is common among arena-shy horses who freeze during their performance. They fear that if they show any expression, they may get it wrong and be in disgrace, so they shut down and lose athleticism. Working though the exercises and giving lots of yeses and fewer nos will soon restore their confidence. By

⬆ Whiskers prefers to work near other horses, so Jemima is teaching her to be more confident when she is on her own. At first Whiskers spins around and naps, trying to get back to the group

⬆ Jemima asks her positively and firmly to continue to move away and as soon as she does removes the annoying pressure of her aids and body language. Whisker's body language shows she is still protesting

⬆ They begin to do some good work and have some soak time on a long rein. Jemima will have to be prepared to repeat this schooling several times during the session

⬇ If a horse jibs and tries to rear, quickly turn him and keep moving his feet on a small circle until he is gentle. Then ask him to do several transitions and turns to ensure your leadership has been accepted

⟨ Using a leapfrog-style game, Roger and Joanna work on having their horses stay calm and polite. One horse overtakes the other and moves off and the horse that is left behind is asked to accept this and stay calm. This work can progress to more challenging manoeuvres including one horse going out of sight of the other. It can be used in hand and is excellent for children's ponies

cultivating and clarifying the 'buttons' (p.42) you will remove any confusion and probably find the problem resolves itself as your timing and skills improve and your horse's trust respect and confidence in your leadership grows.

Emergency measures: Keep pressure on the horse all the time he is not doing what you want and instantly release and reward him only when he starts to do what you do want, which means you may do a lot of stopping and starting. Just remember each time he stops is not a failure but an opportunity to school him to go forward when requested. Be careful you are not rewarding the horse for napping by releasing the pressure at the wrong moment; this is a very common bad timing fault. You need to get your timing quicker than his, so that you stop him before he stops you by napping. Use plenty of tight circles when he naps and then offer him the opportunity to move straight in the right direction. Remember you must be moving his feet, not him moving yours – napping is when the horse manages to reverse this role successfully. It is more important that he inches along in the required direction and receives loads of praise for every inch, than that he gallops along in the wrong direction. Consistently persist in your ask and reward and you will eventually be successful.

Long-term solutions: You need to work through the Effective Training exercises. Thought reversal training works wonders here, too. Beginning in hand, have the horse do some hard work at the stables and then offer him the chance to come away from them a short way, where you should allow him to rest. Repeat repeat, repeat and build up on the distance until he

looks forward to leaving the stables, and doesn't feel so desperate to get back to the safety of them.

You also need to educate him that the stable is not the only haven from the rigours of the world. There are other places he can rest and relax with you, and mow the grass too! Once this is going well in hand, do the same work ridden. If he hurries back to the stable then again make being close to the stable a place of hard work and being away restful, allowing him to graze under a distant tree or similar. You can also do this work if the horse naps when asked to leave the lorry or other horses. Make being where you do want him rewarding and being where you don't want him hard work.

If he naps by galloping back towards the stables (or lorry) turn him and go the other way and only allow him to continue homeward when he is gentle. If he rushes turn him away again and continue training in the same way as you did at the stables. Begin with working in hand and progress back to ridden when all his Effective Training buttons are established (see p.42) and he is easier to control.

Pitfalls: remember that you must not release the pressure and reward the horse by stroking and soothing him while he is napping, then when he stops napping chase him along until he naps again. That's no reward for trying, is it? But how often do you see this done?

⟡ Veronica trains an anxious young horse to lead from the stable to the school and the school to the stable without napping or hurrying. They go to and fro until the horse has developed a good measure of self-control and is ready to ride safely

• Spooking

Often a horse is not genuinely afraid of the object he shies at, he may be checking up on your leadership skills and just trying to move your feet, probably successfully! He may be keen to change your focus and create a crisis as an evasion from something he doesn't want to do, such as work that is tedious, too demanding or frightening. It's a bit like him distracting you by saying, 'Hey! Look over there!' and then making good his escape. Horses especially do this if they feel that their rider is being predatorial or hopelessly weak; in either case they feel their survival depends on escaping or reasserting themselves as the leader. The task is to reverse the scenario. Reread the information about leadership and partnership (p.18), and do the exercises in section 2 (pp.54–113). Exercises for particular problems are listed below.

Here are a few further tips for coping with spooking. Whatever you do, don't get angry and beat your horse because you will destroy any trust you had gained. You will cease to be a respected leader and become the dreaded predator. It is essential to remain detached from both your horse's and your own fears and emotions. If he makes you angry or scared, get him home with as little interaction with you as possible. Ask someone else to take care of him for the moment and don't go near him again until you are in a fit state of mind to be worthy of his respect. Then address the issue and begin reschooling.

When you are working on spooking first try to understand why your horse is doing it and use this information to adopt a schooling strategy to overcome it. Is it:

• because he is genuinely fearful of something? Respond with reassuring leadership and confidence-building spook-busting work (exercises 1 to 5, 7, 19, 20).

⭐ Remaining emotionally detached from Gregory's fears, Daisy asks for a softening yield with her right leg. Soon he accepts her leadership and trusts her that the 'lions' are not dangerous

▷ By flexing the horse laterally, Nick Gauntlett controls where his horse's face points and therefore influences, and ultimately controls, where he looks, reducing the possibility of a spook

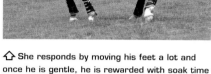

⬆ She responds by moving his feet a lot and once he is gentle, he is rewarded with soak time

⬆ Although his tail is still quite rude, his head is low and soft, indicating that Joanna's leadership has been restored and he feels he can trust her

⬆ Konker tries to take the leadership role, moving Joanna's feet by shying and spinning

• because he wants to have you look where he chooses? Respond with focus-control work (exercises 1 to 7, 9, 10, 19, 20).

• because he wants to move your feet thereby reasserting himself as leader? Respond with feet-moving work (exercises 1, 2, 3, 7, 8, 11, 19, 20).

➡ Being away from home makes horses more cautious. Here The Colt is wary of spectators at a local dressage show. Joanna asks him to yield and move his feet and he soon settles. Accepting the spectators and their picnic within a few moments

⬆ Roger develops Passion's trust in him by asking her to step onto strange surfaces, which are perfectly safe

⬇ Daisy's young mare, Flo, is ready for more advanced spookbusting work. The position of her feet indicates that she is ready to flee, so this work needs careful progression

• because he wants to raise your adrenaline thereby controlling your emotions? Respond with detachment from both his and your own emotions (exercises 1, 2, 5, 7, 11,12, 20).

• because he wants to drop behind the leg? Respond with go-button work (exercises 2, 3, 5, 6, 12, 13, 14).

• because he cannot see the way past the spook? Respond with spookbusting and focus-control work (exercises 1 to 6, 7, 8, 10, 12, 14,18, 20)

This list shows that if you want a fearless horse you need to put time in to develop a partnership of trust and respect by working through the Effective Training exercises. It is essential to control your emotions. Work on the issue, don't avoid it. Spooking is often a fear of being dominated and forced close to scary things; you can achieve great progress through developing your physical and emotional focus and helping your horse to find a way past the spook. This is easier if you have developed your partnership.

◁ Consistent use of pressure and release, along with good timing will help the horse to solve the puzzle set by the rider's aids. This work overcomes the horse's need to shy by establishing trust in and respect for the rider's leadership – Lizzie's horse does not shy at spooks as Lizzie shows her the way through them

Long-term solutions: To help overcome spooking anywhere, imagine riding a line through a complex of cross-country fences, especially skinnies and arrowheads all further complicated by the surrounding crowd and the spray of the water, and adopt the same focus that you would use to ride straight through this combination. Direct the horse through the easiest route. Practise by building pretend fences (poles on the ground will do) at home and putting out' spooks' as well. See exercise 20. Introducing work in narrow spaces will help enormously, too (see p.148). If you and your horse are sufficiently advanced, you can begin to ask for control of where he looks by using lateral flexion off the inside leg bend button and when he gets good at this and if he is trusting you can avoid him looking at the scary object at all. Use block and allow strategies to show the horse exactly where to go.

Pitfalls: If you are always telling your horse where to go and what to do he may relinquish some of his ability to think for himself, so balance this controlled work with times when he has to look after himself and you, such as fun pole or grid work, jumping steeplechase or simple cross-country fences, hacking out or hunting, even riding on a free rein to carry you safely crossing open land or varied terrain. This work develops his sense of self-preservation as well as your and his balance and self-carriage.

⇨ JP and Syd both focus straight ahead

• Poor halts and not standing still

To halt calmly and stand still, on the bit, in a competition arena is emotionally very difficult for a horse and he must have great trust in you to do it well. Horses do not naturally stand up square for long and will rest a hind leg or move a front foot. They often keep one foot ahead ready to flee, and for the horse to square up and 'park' for you takes training. Before you begin training work be aware that not standing still can also be a sign of a discomfort from a crooked rider, a sore back or an uncomfortable saddle. Check this is not why if your horse is a fidget before you embark on retraining him by working through the Effective Training exercises.

Long-term solutions: If your horse is respectful of your space, trusts your leadership and easily allows you to move and control his feet (that is, he is particularly good at exercises 2, 9 and 16), then your work will be simple. You need to learn to feel where your horse's feet are and count them into the halt making sure all four are well placed – without having to look. An amazing number of riders can be seen peering down to count the feet, which is not only extremely uncomfortable for the horse, but also unbalances him. On a hard surface – so you can hear – practise listening and feeling where his feet are. If you find it impossible then have an 'eye on the ground' to tell you. The best training for the rider for this is a solid 2 x 1m (6ft x 3ft) board with rubber matting on it (to prevent it becoming slippery). Train the horse in hand to halt with all four feet on the board squarely and easily (see exercise 9), then progress to doing the same ridden, going through the paces as appropriate.

⬆ Daisy has almost achieved a perfect square halt with Gregory. He has slightly fallen onto his forehand but his feet are square and his energy is held under him and he is alert but still

This is fun to do and brilliant training for both horse and rider. Once this is in place try just with just a mark on the ground. Make your downward transition using a light seat to free up his back. He needs time to get organized and it is your responsibility, as his leader, to make it as easy as possible for him to be successful.

When a horse is asked to stand still and doesn't, every movement he makes is moving the rider's feet – leadership issues become important again. Apply the thought-changing process so you keep moving his feet around in circles and turns and then when you think he is ready for a rest, ask him if he would like to stand still. If he does, reward him with a 'yes', but be sure you move him off before he moves you again. Good timing is required! Keep repeating this and he will learn to prefer to stand still and have his rub, especially if you sit as lightly as possible on his back, to having to keep on walking in tiny circles and turns. In the end standing still will become his preferred choice.

⬇ I am training Konker to place his feet square on this mat.

⬆ The Colt is attempting to evade all Joanna's aids in all directions. She continues to ask him to bend until he comes willingly between hand and leg aids again, which she rewards before work starts again

• Resistance to the bit

A horse that is very set in his neck, poll and jaw may have developed a habit of resistance or may be uncomfortable somewhere in his body. Have him checked out before you try to make him flex. Working through the Effective Training exercises will teach him how to find release from pressure and you can use this to teach him how to flex (see exercise 15 in particular). Remember, you ask for flexion at the poll once he is ready to work on the bit, and then you are seeking to have his poll as the highest point with his face vertical. If he is still not truly balanced and working in soft, forward, self-carriage he is not ready for working with direct flexion yet.

Overbending This is a complex problem and the solution is often difficult to find. If the cause is overuse of draw reins, which force horses to flex their neck, you need to re-educate the horse to flex just his poll (see exercise 15). Ask him always to carry his poll as the highest point. This takes a lot of retraining work; the horse will also need time to redevelop the correct muscles.

⬇⬇ If a horse is braced, flexion is more easily learnt by asking for yield in hand. Ask for a step back at the same time as asking for flexion at the poll. Joanna gives Jill's legs a tap to help her move back (below)

Behind the bit If the horse is seeking to be behind the bit, check you are not blocking him, try changing to a milder bit or even try working without one for a while. Ask him to maintain a contact with a soft following hand and ensure he is not dropping behind the leg as well. Ensure your body is allowing him to soften in his jaw, and that you are not blocking him. School though the Effective Training exercises, especially 14.

Leaning on the bit If the horse is leaning on the bit then go through the Effective Training exercises to help him find his balance and confirm through training that pressure on his mouth means he should slow down his feet (see exercises 2, 9 and 17). Make sure his poll flexion button feels different to his slow button, that your position is not driving him onto the forehand or that any tension in you is not interfering with him.

Above the bit Some horses escape control by raising their head and pushing out through the chest underneath the rider's rein. By doing this they evade slowing down in response to pressure on the stop button in their mouth. Reschooling using the Effective Training exercises will cultivate his correct response to the stop button. To help him learn not to brace against his rider, and because pulling back on his head only increases the problem, try flexing him laterally to achieve some softening. Maintain that bend until he slows his feet, and only then allow him to go straight, when he is not raising his head and pushing out through the chest.

Wrong bend and poor lateral flexion This resistance can also be a bad habit or a physiological problem, so get him checked over first. Work through the Effective Training exercises, especially 10, and make the horse's work easier by always asking for the neck and shoulder to yield out before asking for the ribs to bend. Horses can drop on their inside shoulders to block you and can also use their ribs to stiffen against you, so work on their buttons as well their trust and respect.

HEAD-CARRIAGE

Horses naturally carry their heads level and low with most of their weight on their forehand. Training is needed to teach them to engage their hindquarters to support the weight of the heavy forehand in order to be able to raise and round their backs and withers before they can comfortably carry their heads higher, otherwise they will just hollow their backs and lose their athletic ability and balance.

⬆ The Colt is above the bit and pushing hard through Joanna's hand and being strong and rude, which is unacceptable

⬆ She asks him to halt and stand with a little lateral bend, which he does. Alternatively, she could ask him to leg yield and come gentle to her aids and then circle quietly until he is staying soft enough to continue politely

• Running away from the aids

When a horse tries to escape from the aids it may be because he has been successful with this before or that the aids have been too strong or given for too long. Going through the Effective Training exercises will help him to relearn how to feel the aid and follow that feel (see exercise 14). This is usually quite simple to teach once you realize what is happening, but it takes many repeats to establish.

To make sure the horse waits for the aid and doesn't anticipate or try to guess it, be prepared to change your mind at the last second. For example, prepare to trot from walk, then if the horse anticipates going into trot, politely remain in walk. The same applies with work in hand.

• Pulling, especially across country

Pulling is very rude and can be caused by the horse's bad balance or a lack of understanding of the rider's aids, confusion over the rider's wishes or a desensitized mouth. Many horses that pull are unable or unwilling to carry their own weight over their own feet and depend of the rider's hand for balance.

⬆ Greg on Whisky and Roger on The Colt. Both horses and riders are well balanced; the horses are rounded in their backs, using their belly muscles well

Long-term solutions: Pulling is easily improved by going back to basics. The early Effective Training exercises will help with balance problems. How well does your horse understand the aids? Remember, to a horse, there is no logical reason why pulling at a bit shoved into his mouth should mean slow your feet down. Go back to exercises 2, 9, 14 and 17 and re-establish that when you give a body statement and then put pressure on his mouth you want him to slow his feet down. Don't release the pressure on his mouth until the moment he does stop his feet, then respond quickly, instantly releasing the pressure, and reward him with a little soak time before repeat, repeat, repeat.

Only when this is really good in walk, trot and canter can you begin to ask for the same thing from the gallop (see above) or jumping. Even at this speed, remember the body language to tell him your intention. Imagine you are galloping up to a cliff edge and you *must* stop. Don't fall over the edge!

There is much confusion between asking a horse to check and give more engagement from behind, and asking the horse to slow down across country. Checking is a fast half halt and engages the hind end and rebalances; slowing down is different and the horse should respond by slowing his speed, his momentum and his feet, but still engaging his hindquarters. This needs to be trained separately (see exercises 2, 9 and 17).

⬆ Joanna repeats this work every time The Colt is rude until he understands that she wants him to stay polite, balanced and soft and that she doesn't intend to become involved in a tugging match, quietly reasserting herself as his leader

• Behind the leg, lazy, refusing, running out

As with napping, being behind the leg is very rude. Rather like the napping work (p.130), retraining may mean a lot of starting and stopping because the horse needs to learn to keep going on his own until he is told to change pace or halt. By working through the Effective Training exercises, especially 6b (p.72), you will re-educate the 'go' button and develop a much more willing horse. Do as many simple upward transitions as it takes, starting from halt to walk. Be sure you are giving a good forward-going body statement, softening the arm and hand and taking pressure off the 'go' button the moment he moves for you. Initially, he will probably stop again and you will have to repeat it again and again. Ask him to keep going on his own until he walks several strides and then a whole circuit of the arena without you having to remind him to keep going! Then you can get more ambitious and try halt to trot and trot on.

Eventually you are seeking to go from halt to canter and canter on at the press of a leg or even just from the body statement. If he is slow off the leg or fails to try to stay in front of your leg, use a flappy stick on the shoulder or just behind your leg at the same time, to sharpen him up. Check that your hands or body language are not blocking or resisting forward movement. It is quite common for people to be trying to ride their horse forward with the handbrake left on, remember he can only guess what you want from your body language and aids. It is essential to ask politely with the aids and build up pressure levels (see p.51) only if necessary.

Horses will only offer to expend as much effort as you demand and offer appreciation for. Often they have sussed out their rider and how much of the work they can get the rider to do for them! Don't allow yourself to be kicking away at every stride while the horse slops along doing none of the work.

⬆ Gregory has fallen behind the leg so Daisy asks him to bring his energy forward again

⬆ He is reluctant so she uses little taps with the schooling whip at the same time as repeating the request with her leg to tickle him up

⬆ He responds well and after a few moments of accepting and acknowledging his effort with some good forward work...

⬆ ...she rewards him with a rest. By repeating the request, accepting and rewarding the try, Gregory learns to stay willingly in front of the leg

• Scared of water jumps

A horse is fearful of jumping into water because he knows instinctively that it is risky to allow his feet to get into any situation he cannot flee from. A horse really does think there may be danger lurking in the depths. As his trust and confidence in his rider's decisions and leadership grows so his fears will subside. We cannot force him to trust us. Trust is built up by using strategies to prove you are trustworthy, will never revert to predatorial behaviour and will consistently make good decisions on behalf of your horse for his well being.

Long-term solutions: Plenty of preparatory training is required to gain his trust and respect; exercises 2, 4, 5, 6 and 9 are especially useful. If you have already worked through all the exercises you will have overcome most of the schooling and leadership issues that make your horse resistant to your

⬆ ⬇ Roger puts pressure on Whisky and blocks all her resistances until she walks onto the board. Yes, thanks. His hand is yielding to allow her to move freely

◁ Joanna's focus gives The Colt confidence to pop straight over the drop into the water – good boy

⬆ Konker is being trained to accept the tarpaulin under his feet, which is good preparation for walking through water

requests. Should he still be worried you need to prove to him that you are worthy of his trust by doing more pressure and release work with transitions and turns. Also re-establish good responses to all the buttons, especially the go button.

Once these controls are all in place, begin working with water by asking him to walk into a simple splash – in hand to start with, if possible. (Be careful that there is no risk of the leadrope catching in the wing of the jump.)

Use your judgement. If he is still fearful, go back a few steps and, using advance and retreat, ask him to walk onto and over a heavy board or tarpaulin (see exercise 9). Only when he is fully confident doing this should you ask him just to look at the water,

⬆ Roger encourages Charlie to be brave through water, ready to do it with his young rider on board ...

⬆ ... and the training has paid off – Sophie and Charlie enjoy a splash

then approach one step at a time. Continue with a persistent ask and as he moves each step, instantly stop asking and say 'Yes! Thanks, but please stay here, don't back away.' Repeat the ask, move, thanks – step by step until he is quite close, then take him away for a break for a few minutes before deciding whether that is enough progress for today or whether to continue the training. Your judgement is crucial in deciding how far and fast to progress. Eventually having progressed to the edge of the water, work as with napping (see p.130) to make stepping in the water a nice place to be and sticking outside the water a less pleasant place to be. This is thought-reversal work and takes time but is worth it if you want to retrain an established problem.

⬆ Pudding enjoys a cooling paddle, well on the way to becoming a fearless little pony

⬇ Roger and a four-year-old he is schooling boldly go into the water with good focus and balance, developing confidence

At competitions

One of the most common reasons owners come to us is because their horse is finding it difficult to cope with the stress of shows and competitions. Usually, it is not the competing that is the problem, but more being away from home and the general range and amount of activity that goes on at shows. Brass bands, clapping crowds, PA systems, carriage driving and hound parades and birds of prey displays are just some of the things that the competition horse has to deal with.

There are plenty of ways that you can prepare your horse for the sights and sounds of competition beforehand; especially useful are Effective Training exercises 17, 18, 19 and 20.

• Clapping and crowdproofing

If you are planning on going to competitions add the following exercise to your list of things in preparation. Gather together as many people as you can, to be an 'audience', and explain to them that they need to respond instantly to your instructions to start or stop clapping, to clap quietly, louder, or to stand still or move about and so on – practise this with them before you bring in the horse because getting the timing right is essential.

Prepare your horse quietly by working through your Effective Training exercises until he is gentle and trusting, allowing you control of all four feet. Ensure that you have included making the smallest

⬆ Daisy carries a bunch of flowers and manages Gregory one-handed, using her legs to steer, at our training prizegiving

circle possible and leg yield on the circle (exercise 11) so that you can use either of these to move his feet and calm him if he gets nervous. This will reassure him that you are his worthy leader and he can trust you to take good care of him, even if he is a bit scared. Make sure you have your hat, gloves and boots and carry a good stick to push him away from you if needed.

⬆ Parades of hounds frequently take place before prizegivings so be prepared to participate or evacuate in good time

SUDDEN NOISES

Along with seeing scary objects, noise is a very common cause of spooking. Horses have very sensitive hearing and today's loud world can worry the bravest. They will frequently run away from loud noises, especially motorbikes, low-flying aircraft and gunshots. The arena work (above) will help your horse, as will the Effective Training exercises, but also practise introducing noises and gradually increasing their suddenness, using advance and retreat techniques to progress.

If your horse takes fright and runs from a loud noise when you are riding, grab one rein and try to turn him in circles until he settles, only allowing him to go forward when he is calm and gentle. Wear high visibility clothing to help pilots, drivers and shooters to see you early enough to avoid any unexpected 'training opportunities'!

With the audience grouped in one area and you leading the horse some distance away, start with quiet clapping. If the horse remains gentle, ask the audience to stop clapping, and reward him. If he is nervous, keep them clapping quietly while you move his feet (as described above) to reassert yourself as his leader. It is important that the audience keeps on clapping gently until you say stop – you are the one who can feel if he is trying to accept the clapping or if he is still braced and trying to tell the audience to stop clapping. Big difference! You are his trainer, so you need to decide what he is thinking. Once he does, relax, reward him, enjoy a little soak time before repeat, repeat, repeat.

Gradually increase the noise and the closeness of the audience until he can stand right beside them with them all clapping and cheering and moving around; then have him move around them, too. Progress through the stages carefully, repeating each stage at least twice as sometimes horses find it harder the second time. Repeat the work until you feel he's totally confident with all types of clapping. He should be able to work at any speed, including medium canter, and remain gentle. Be prepared for this to take more than one session – ask your friends to return again to help soon. I hope we didn't lead you to think this training is a quick fix! It really is well worth it when you end up with a fearless horse.

To be able to have everyone clapping, cheering and moving around the horse, stopping and starting suddenly and getting as close as possible to him while he continues to work brilliantly in all paces, you and your helpers need good timing to avoid training the horse to panic by mistake (see p.40). When your horse can remain calm surrounded by clapping supporters you will be able to lead the parade into the main ring enjoying their accolade and your horse won't turn a hair!

⬆ If you have experienced a problem, don't avoid the issue but reschool the horse as soon as possible. Here Lorna and Gym focus forward well when approaching the water jump.

⇨ Pippa and Primmore's Pride do it for real – winning the World Cup at Chatsworth in 2004. Note the rosette tails, carefully tucked away from Primmore's Pride's eyes

↑ Plenty of pre-preparation will give everyone confidence. Make use of any chances you get to work in the practice ring, and wear your competition kit to enable your horse to get used to the tails flapping on his back

↑ Don't freeze with nerves at competitions, instead take every opportunity to move your horse's feet to give him confidence in your leadership

• Arena shyness and stage fright

Even experienced horses can develop competition nerves and may become arena shy. They may be anxious during parades and trot ups, and may shy or be fearful near people, especially in groups, such as audiences. You may have experienced a loss of performance when you compete and you may feel your horse tensing up, especially in the main ring. The horse may feel threatened by the crowd, especially if it is in tiered seating, cutting off his peripheral vision and possible escape routes. If the work he does in the ring is exciting or difficult, that would add to his anxiety, as would adrenaline raised while on parade or galloping around after winning. This might be especially marked when you re-enter the ring because he might think he has successfully 'escaped' from the clapping.

If your own pulse rate rises, your horse will feel this and interpret it as a sign of danger. Try to learn to control it maybe through breathing work, yoga or tai chi. Beware of becoming predatorial if you are up tight. Remain detached from your emotions and your horse's fears: you are the leader. School him through

↑ Remain detached from your emotions – go out and do the job you have trained to do. Show how well you can do it

his anxiety and ask him to become gentle, soft and forward by moving his feet a lot.

Emergency measures: If you have unexpected problems at a competition, try walking your horse in small circles. If you have been using the Effective Training exercises, he will find this a reassuringly familiar safety zone. If he is bracing and resisting then don't become confrontational, instead use some yielding work, such as bending, leg yielding, shoulder in, transitions and turns. All these will help him soften and accept your leadership as you regain control of his feet. Horses will often settle if you ride accurate patterns and repeat them as this, too, is effective control of their feet. It is vital that you always look up and around and about and remain relaxed to tell the horse you have checked all the 'tigers' out there and they are harmless. You should also be very aware of all the possible hazards in the ring and give them as wide a berth as possible. Never try to force the horse to go close to the 'tigers'; this is confrontational and predatorial behaviour and may damage his confidence in your judgement.

The worst things you can do are to become aggressive with him or inadvertently reward a horse for his prey-like behaviour by freezing and failing to offer any leadership when he is panicking. There is a big difference between a reassuring rub and nervous patting. Think of being involved in an accident. Who would you take your leadership from – or find most reassuring – the kindly person who is stroking your arm or the more assertive and effective one, organizing an ambulance to get you to the hospital? The latter I suspect. Your horse feels the same; when he is scared and in a crisis, he needs help in the form of strong calm leadership.

DRESS REHEARSALS

If the quality of your horse's work deteriorates when he gets into the ring, he is probably arena shy and you need to try to get some practice in the ring: either appeal to the authorities to let you go in after the competition has finished, or go to some competitions just for training purposes. Even some of the top events allow riders to walk their horse into the main ring for half an hour on the day before the competition starts. This is a wonderful preparation opportunity, so grab the chance to familiarize your horse with the surroundings he will be competing in. Check what the stewards are happy for you to do, and be very careful not to contravene any rules and get eliminated. Usually you are only allowed to walk in straight lines so walk and halt transitions with lateral flexion will be your only chance to move his feet. Should you get the chance to work-in there or nearby, do a lot of moving of feet with lateral work and turns and transitions with the horse being soft and going forward. For us lesser mortals, riding clubs and pony clubs are usually very helpful and, if you ask politely, may allow you to use their arenas for schooling, especially if you offer to help dismantle them at the end of the show; sometimes the judges, will even offer to stay in their cars and advise you. Accept graciously!

Long-term solutions: The best solution to these difficulties is to retrain your horse using the Effective Training exercises, particularly exercise 20, and the techniques suggested for crowdproofing (p.144). Do this work at home as you need to have control of the stimuli to help the horse to overcome his fear and trust his rider. It takes considerably longer to reschool a horse that has been frightened than it does to train a trusting horse to accept these things before being over-faced by them. Once a horse gets a fright, he will have lost some confidence in human leadership, so you need to revise the relevant exercises.

◁ Keeping good rhythmic breathing and turning your head are two ways to check that you have not become frozen in fear yourself

• Fear of confined spaces

Fear of containment may show itself in stables, start boxes or stalls, narrow walkways, horseboxes, and trailers. It is usually more evident when the situation has already raised adrenaline levels, such as riding into the cross country start box, because everyone is excited and the combination of the two things is very confrontational and intimidating to the horse, who prefers wide open spaces. His mother taught him never to get trapped anywhere!

⬆ The Colt, who had never been in a trailer before, shows the benefits of Effective Training at a Le Trec competition

Emergency measures: If you need to get him in there instantly, the best strategy is to yield him gradually towards the 'trap' and if possible, such as with a start box, go through it a few times before asking him to wait in it. And when you do walk into it keep yielding and moving him even if it is only changing his flexion. Avoid letting him stop or plant his feet. With a start box, on 'go', try to go gently because it is often the violence of a standing start that frightens the horse in the first place. If the consequences of his agreeing to trust you enough to go into the start box are unpleasant or alarming for him, he will be even more reluctant next time.

⬇ Daisy trains Flo in a simulated start box. First she asks her to leave in walk, building up to canter, always calming her with low adrenaline. It is the suddenness of a standing start that fires up the adrenaline and creates anxiety

⬆ JP uses show jumps to build a young horse's confidence in tight spaces

Long-term solutions: Remember: quick fixes are only emergency measures to get you through a tricky situation, to train your horse properly you need to build trust, which the exercises in part two will help with. Exercise 8 is especially useful as fear of close spaces is often related to a fear of getting the feet trapped. Overcome a specific fear by working on remaining gentle and soft in increasingly smaller spaces. Use cardboard boxes, blocks or dust sheets to create the spaces as they won't hurt the horse if he touches them. Using advance and retreat progress from one box to a whole pen made of boxes, blocks,

⬆ Konker has progressed from his earlier work (p.44) and now steps through the blocks happily

dust sheets. Remember to keep the pressure on when he is doing what you don't what and take it off instantly when he is doing what you do want. Eventually, you can start to use poles and blocks or jump stands – as long as there is no danger of him panicking and crashing into them. Finally, use your props to make start boxes, walkways or whatever it is he was worried about, out in the field. For problems with start boxes, remember to practise your gentle starts, too.

• At the finish

Horses are often surprisingly hard to manage at the finish of a race or event as they are bursting with adrenaline, struggling to get their breath, sweating profusely and probably weary. They need to be cooled quickly, but make sure no one takes the bridle off the horse until he is calmer. Clip a rope onto the bit to give you something longer to lead him by until then. Many events have a paddock with shade and wash off areas, but the horse may well resist being near them. This is only because his adrenaline is high, if possible allow him to walk in circles while he cools off. If you have done your preparatory training the horse will be trusting, confident and easy to control, but if he has had none of this training you may need to move his feet quite assertively to establish your leadership. Halt and moving him back and forward are often the only options now, and you may need to use strong body language to be effective. The previous work you have done with pressure and release will have taught you how to cope, without distressing the horse. This training is invaluable for all competitors – horses, grooms, riders, trainers, owners, children, mothers and all!

CAN YOUR HORSE PASS THE 'UNCLE GEORGE' TEST?

The ultimate test of your training is to pretend to be 'Uncle George': a bad horseman and made all the worse by being drunk. In your absence he helps himself to your horse. He trips over when approaching the horse and clings onto the horse's leg to pull himself up. He then flings his arm around the poor horse's neck and pats him furiously on the neck while peering into

⬆ Julie builds Konker's confidence using in-hand work – in this case tapping on his side

his eye and shouting 'good boy'. He then proceeds to tack up the horse and scramble on with the saddle slipping, ending up sitting behind the saddle. Once he manages to sit upright in the saddle, he sets off at the trot with only one stirrup and jumps the little garden gate into the paddock. Your wonderfully trained horse tolerates all this gently and kindly and when Uncle George finally slithers off and lies in a drunken stupor on the grass, your angelic horse just grazes quietly until he is rescued on your return. These are all the things a horse naturally hates but with adequate training and trust in humans he will learn to tolerate almost anything – even Uncle George.

◁ Accustoming a horse to accept the rider in an odd position so that he learns to remain calm if a rider falls off

APPRECIATE YOUR HORSE

You have probably read through this section because you've had some difficulties with your horse. Take heart, all riders and owners have problems with their horses from time to time. Remember that the most difficult horses to train are often also the most brilliant because they are the natural leaders and would not have made the mistake of getting eaten by lions – the ever-present natural selection of survival of the fittest. However, even if your horse is not the most brilliant performer, if he is just a family friend or the children's beloved pony, spend time with him and enjoy him. Horses are wonderful creatures to be with and have the capacity to bring great joy to those who love them.

⇨ Horses are wonderful creatures and bring great joy...

Acknowledgments

There are so very many people and horses that have enhanced our lives made this book possible and we would like to acknowledge them all, but will have to select just a few to thank here. Our horses have been our teachers, especially The Colt, but we would like to express our appreciation to all the teachers who shared their knowledge with us. I should like to begin with the late Sgt. Ben Jones who taught me with the Portman Pony Club and Mrs Molly Sivewright who encouraged me

to watch and learn. Mrs Nicole Bartle who was painstakingly thorough in her dressage training in preparation for my BHSI, a wonderful foundation for which I am forever grateful, Hank van Bergen who helped us prepare Primmore Hill for Badminton with his sympathetic and effective teaching that we have never forgotten. More recently, Monty Roberts, Richard Maxwell, Charlotte Dennis, Mark Rodney and Chris Irwin for their horsemanship that has inspired us. Also the British team trainers Yogi Breisner, Ken Clawson and Tracey Robinson for giving us the opportunity to watch, listen and learn from them and latterly Perry Wood for encouraging us to communicate better and showing Roger that he too can enjoy dressage!

For *The Fearless Horse* we have to thank Kate Green for starting us off and David & Charles for giving us the opportunity – Jane, Jo, Jennifer and Jodie have been so helpful and supportive throughout. The patient rider models and their wonderful horses deserve lots of thank you's for allowing us to photograph their training sessions: Julie Garbutt with Konker, Caroline and John Peter Daker with Bow House Sidney and others, Daisy Binding with Do The Right Thing and Flo, Jemima Baker and Whiskers, Sophie and Jasmine Walker with Charlie and Pudding, Rachel Shire and Buddy, also Rachel Parsons and June Rowland for their groundwork, and not least Passion and The Colt. We are also grateful to the skilled photographers Fiona Scott Maxwell, Felicity Chandler and Matt Roberts. The horses were the stars, of course, especially The Colt whom we had to tempt to show us just how bad he could be, which was upsetting for all of us, and who then so forgivingly allowed us to regain his trust and respect – generosity indeed. Our journey of learning continues.

Pippa Funnell has kindly allowed us to use photographs of her riding Primmore's Pride to illustrate this book. We are most grateful to her for this as she is such a brilliant rider and horse trainer, and he is our beloved mare Primmore Hill's most famous progeny. We have not been involved with Primmore's Pride's training in any way since selling him as a foal. We much admire the way Pippa has produced him so successfully from the start, as she does all her horses, the sign of a true horsewoman. Pippa has given us much encouragement with this book but is not associated with our Effective Training or this book in any way. Our thanks go also to Primmore's Pride's owners Roger and Denise Lincoln who have shared his triumphs with us so generously. To breed a champion is every breeder's dream, and we thank them all for making our dream come true.

Picture Credits

Felicity Chandler pages 12 14 (lower series), 26 (left), 30 (left) 38, 39 (series) 54 (top), 57 (lower), 61 (top, both), 69, 95, 98 (left), 109 (lower), 122, 135 (top) 143, 145 (top), 148 (top)

Roger and Joanna Day pages 5 (lower), 7 (top), 10 (top), 11 (lower), 12 (left), 23 (right), 24 (top left, lower left), 47 (top right), 48, 49 (lower), 54 (lower left and right), 55, 56 (top and middle right), 57 (right), 69 (lower right), 84, 89 (top right), 95 (left), 106 (right), 108 (right), 111 (middle), 112 (right), 113 (lower left), 120 (lower right), 121 (lower left), 123 (top), 124 (all), 129 (right top, middle, lower), 131 (lower), 133 (middle, lower), 143 (lower), 144 (lower), 146 (top right), 148 (top left and right), 149 (top), 151

Mike Freeman page 112 (right) and front cover

Suze Ingle page 109 (top)

Andrew Morton pages 1, 114 (lower right)

Peter Ayres Photography page 5 (top left)

Helen Revington pages 4, 19 (middle, lower right), 107 (lower left)

Fiona Scott-Maxwell pages 7 (top), 10 (lower right), 15 (lower left), 17 (lower right), 18 (lower and top), 20 (left), 21 (top and lower), 22 (two lower), 23 (left), 31 (top), 41 (top and lower left, lower right), 44 (top, middle and lower right), 56 (left), 60, 66 (top), 77, 79 (lower right), 82 (lower right), 85 (right), 89 (lower left and right), 94, 99 (lower left), 100 (lower left and right), 101 (top left, middle and right), 102 (right), 103 (left), 105 (lower right), 109 (lower right) 112 (left), 113 (top and middle left), 115, 117 (lower), 118 (right sequence), 123 (lower), 132 (right), 135 (lower), 137 (lower left and right), 145 (lower), 146 (left, lower right), 147, 149 (lower)

Steven Sparks page 107

Western Morning News page 5 (top right)

About the authors

Roger & Joanna Day are well known in the eventing world, having bred top horses for many years, the most successful being Primmore's Pride, winner of the Kentucky three-day event in 2003 and twice winner of Badminton Horse Trials. Joanna is a British Horse Society Instructor and British Eventing Accredited Trainer. Roger is a recently retired British Eventing Regional Director and continues to work as an FEI steward.

www.fearlesshorse.co.uk

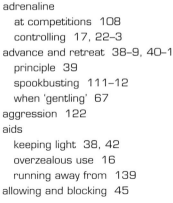

Index